SPRING IN WASHINGTON

ILLUSTRATIONS BY FRANCIS L. JAQUES

FOREWORD BY ROGER TORY PETERSON

NEW YORK 1963

SPRING
IN
WASHINGTON

BY

LOUIS J. HALLE

ATHENEUM

The author wishes to thank *Audubon Magazine* for permission
to include in this book an abbreviated version of "The Spotted
Thrushes," which appeared in the January-February, 1943, issue.

Published by Atheneum
Reprinted by arrangement with Harper & Brothers

Copyright 1947, 1957, by Louis J. Halle, Jr.
All rights reserved
Published in Canada by McClelland & Stewart Ltd.
Manufactured in the United States of America by
The Colonial Press Inc., Clinton, Massachusetts

First Atheneum Edition

TO BARBARA

FOREWORD
by Roger Tory Peterson

IN THE YEAR the atomic age was born a young
man on a bicycle appointed himself monitor of
spring in the nation's capital. Starting before sun-up
each morning, he pedaled miles and saw much before
his workday began at the offices of the State Department. That the year was 1945 is of no importance, for
the events he chronicled could have taken place in
1845 or 2045. The rites of spring are eternal.

In 1945 I, too, watched the progress of spring along
the Potomac. I had been stationed for two years at
Fort Belvoir—next door to Lebanon, where Dr. Paul
Bartsch was rebuilding the colonial mansion which has
become the home of his sunset years. In 1946 I again
saw the coming of spring in Washington and again in
1947. Like so many others I expected to be only a brief
resident in the Washington area, but I lingered on
until ten years had elapsed. Ten years gives one time
to know a place. Although I have now moved to Connecticut's green hills I shall always be able to recall
the country roads, and nearly every woodlot, swamp,
or creek within striking distance of the District of
Columbia, as well as each bit of park within the city
itself.

Where is there a walk more lovely in the month of
May than the towpath along the old Chesapeake and
Ohio Canal? Where can one see more warblers on a
good "wave" or where, for that matter, can one find
a greater density of nesting song birds? The nesting
density in the average deciduous woodland in the East,
according to the Audubon breeding-bird censuses, is

four to five birds per acre. The average number per acre along the Potomac near Cabin John runs between fourteen and fifteen! Wild flowers spread their scatter-rugs under the century-old sycamores; blue phlox, wild geraniums, violets, golden ragwort, and scores of others make gardens of the woodland glades. One does not have to be a bird-watcher or a botanist to enjoy the towpath in the spring. Only an insensitive eye would fail to respond to all this color and life.

Rock Creek has a beauty quite different from that of the alluvial Potomac; it is a rock-bound stream hemmed in by low hills and ravines. Its voice is the song of the Louisiana waterthrush, a thin wild cascade of sound half lost in the murmur and rush of running water. Here turkey vultures have roosted on the wooded slopes for nearly a century (1826—John Burroughs) and lately they have been joined by the black vultures which formerly spent their nights along the Potomac. Night herons, too, make their headquarters in Rock Creek Park in the vicinity of the Zoological Gardens. Apartment dwellers on the edge of the park can hear the whooping of barred owls at night and the yapping of foxes.

Across the bridge in Virginia, at the edge of the National Airport, is Roaches Run with its hundreds of wintering pintails. In early spring, before the light green comes back to the willows and the white to dogwoods, it is also a way-stop for gadwalls, baldpates, ruddies, and other northbound ducks. The waterfowl pay little heed to the thundering airliners that sweep up from the landing strips; for was not Roaches Run an airport long before the National Airport was conceived?

Continuing through the colonial town of Alexandria, the Mount Vernon Highway winds southward along the river through lush woodlands where summer tanagers and yellow-throated warblers sing. The bird-watcher parks his car or his bicycle when he comes to the lay-by at Dyke, where a tree-bordered path between cattail marsh and open water arcs into the river. Superficially, Dyke is an attractive marsh, but decade by decade it is growing more sterile, for pollution, the curse of our Eastern rivers, has affected the aquatic life.

Rock Creek, the C. & O. Canal, Roaches Run, and Dyke are among the wild places at the capital's doorstep that Louis Halle writes about in this book. This does not mean that the book applies only to the Washington scene. Its theme is spring, and spring happens to people all around the world. Halle's reflections on this annual miracle might have been written similarly by a Thoreau in New England, a Sigurd Olson in Minnesota, or a John Muir in California. He belongs to that school of writers who know the meaning of wildness and are able to communicate it. To quote a few of his lines:

"It is curious how the preoccupations of the hive fill us, driving out all memory of the universe into which we were born. Perhaps the whole human race may be said to suffer from amnesia, not knowing whence it came or why it finds itself here. . . . We have forgotten that we live in the universe, and that our civilization itself is merely an elaboration of the palm-leaf hat that one of our ancestors tried on ten thousand years ago to ward off the sun, a more complicated and ample version that now not only wards off the sun but shuts out the view. We have lost ourselves within it. Yet some have told me, when I set out to have a look at the stars or to watch the migration of birds, that I was escaping reality."

It is wrong to think of birds and nature as something for odd people who are interested in birds and nature —as Indic philology, perhaps, is only for Indic philologists. Birds and nature represent the basic world in which we live. The observation of them, consequently, is essential to an understanding of that world. It is essential to wisdom.

This thought has a special point in the City of Washington. Perhaps it is no accident that at least four presidents—four of our greatest—George Washington (who lived in the Washington area before the city was founded), Thomas Jefferson, Theodore Roosevelt, and Franklin Roosevelt, were naturalists.

Washington is many things, but two things set it apart from other American cities—its handsome architecture and the trees which make it a city of grace and beauty. L'Enfant, the French designer, had visions of a stately city, reflecting the eighteenth-century Age of Reason. The original plan called for fine buildings enhanced by broad vistas, accentuated by avenues of trees. As the city expanded natural woodlands were set aside to insure breathing spaces. Today we find fingers of woodland (Rock Creek, etc.) still penetrating deep towards the city's heart.

But will Washington always have these breathing spaces? There are city planners today who seem to have forgotten the ideal of beauty and repose. The "improvements" they speak of usually mean the elimination of some park area.

Several years ago, when crossing one of the high bridges over Rock Creek Park, my companion, a newsman from Texas, remarked on "the real estate down there going to waste." When I suggested that natural values or beauty had their place in city planning his only reply was a puzzled stare. How can one convince such people?

Too many men have this blind spot. But thank heavens it is not universal and let us be thankful too that so many of our leaders have been men of vision! More than one president has paraphrased Halle's remark that "men will not take as elevated a view of the national destiny working in the basement of a ware-

house as they will on the heights of an Acropolis." *
If the environment is shabby, the thinking and the
impulses of statesmanship will become shabby.

John Quincy Adams, speaking of Rock Creek Park,
said that after a round of trying official duties as President he would seek relaxation in "this romantic glen,
listening to the singing of a thousand birds. . . ."

Theodore Roosevelt recalled with pleasure that
when he was Chief Executive he often took long walks,
"perhaps down Rock Creek, which was then as wild as
a stream in the White Mountains." Even foreign diplo-
mats have sung the praises of Rock Creek. Viscount
Bryce, the British Ambassador, commented: "What
city in the world is there where a man . . . can within
a quarter of an hour and on his own feet get in a beautiful rocky glen such as you would find in the woods of
Maine or Scotland?"

And yet this park which has served almost as a place
of worship for statesmen has recently been threatened
with a new express highway. There have also been
plans afoot to build a motor-road the length of the
C. & O. Canal, utilizing the bed of this old canal
which was conceived by George Washington and built
for the purpose of opening up the lands beyond the
Appalachian Mountains to settlement and trade.

Inasmuch as men who have borne governmental
responsibilities—from George Washington on—have
found their perspective on human problems enhanced
by getting out and observing the larger world, gaining
refreshment thereby, it is an evil thing to reduce our
capital, certainly America's most beautiful city, to
shabby mediocrity. Washington, alone among the nation's cities, is a national possession.

Washington is a particularly satisfying city for the
naturalist—if he does not mind the humid, almost trop-

* *Washington—City in the Woods.* Audubon Society of the
District of Columbia, 1954.

ical, summer climate. Here the facilities for those of his calling are second to none: wild country at the city's door; vast study collections in the Smithsonian Institution and the National Herbarium; stacks of reference books—some almost priceless—at the Library of Congress; experts by the dozen, all willing to help, in the offices and laboratories of the Fish and Wildlife Service, the National Park Service, the National Forest Service, and the National Museum. Here influential conservation organizations such as the National Wildlife Federation, the Nature Conservancy, the National Parks Association, the Wildlife Management Institute, and the Wilderness Society have their headquarters, as do magazines such as the *National Geographic, Nature, National Parks Magazine, American Forests,* and the *Living Wilderness*. Of the local natural-history societies, the Audubon Society of the District of Columbia is by far the largest with 1200 members. It publishes *The Atlantic Naturalist* and is, perhaps, the most effective local Audubon group in the country.

Edwin Way Teale in his pleasure-giving book, *North With the Spring,* has written of the northward advance of the vernal season across the eastern United States. Unlike Teale, who has dealt with the linear movement of spring in space, Louis Halle deals with it in time. Spring, he points out, is a dramatic transformation of the earth which cannot be said to reach any particular place at any precise moment. It is a series of cumulative events.

Today I read and reread *Spring in Washington* with a particular nostalgia because of my many Washington memories; but let it not be imagined that the book is of only local interest. The birds that Louis Halle writes about are the same birds that sweep northward through half a continent. The laws that govern their behavior are universal laws.

Halle brings to his theme a perception and a simple

beauty of words rarely found outside the writings of Thoreau or Hudson. The black-and-whites by Francis Lee Jaques, who finds it easier to express himself in line and form than by words, are a handsome complement to the text. It is interesting to compare John Burroughs' *Wake Robin,* published in 1871, with *Spring in Washington,* which documents the same scene in the mid-twentieth century. Some things have changed: the city has spread and a few birds like the mockingbird and cardinal have greatly increased. But, regardless of instability in governmental politics and policies, regardless of headline crises, the rhythm of the seasons remains steadfast. As Halle points out, "the discovery of spring each year, is like a rediscovery of the universe."

In a world where so much that is humanly good lives only a moment, it is a source of gratification and comfort that *Spring in Washington* should now, ten years after its first publication, appear in a new edition.

SPRING IN WASHINGTON

I

THOUGH they ransack the National Archives, historians to come will find no records of certain remarkable episodes and developments that took place in Washington during the first half of 1945. The government has no department that takes cognizance of life itself; it posts no watchers out of doors to sniff the wind and inform those within of eternity. That is volunteer work, good occupation for a man. It is not for government personnel, who are preoccupied with official transactions on paper. These are workers in the hive of our civilization, and the hive is their universe. They trouble themselves about the real universe, as Henry Adams puts it, "much as a hive of honey-bees troubles about the ocean, only as a region to be avoided."

A government functionary would not believe you should you tell him that the price of wolfram in Turkey today is not so important as the perennial process of budding and leafing in the neighboring woods. Nevertheless, the opening of the leaves concerned his human ancestors five thousand years ago, though they never heard of buying wolfram, and this alone should give point to what you say. The price of wolfram is not, like the budding of trees, a dependable fact of life. It vanishes from sight in the long perspective; it is excluded from the final reckoning. When the official has completed his operation in the wolfram market he has not really done anything to enrich the life of man or increase his stature; but if he will observe the trees he may preach revelation to remote descendants. I am grateful to Thoreau, who considered himself as a man the superior of any government, for pointing out to me a hundred years ago certain characteristics of the kingfisher that I would otherwise have failed to see. I do not care what he may have paid for eggs, but it is something to stand behind his shoulder and sight the world along his extended arm. Daniel Webster never did as much for me.

To snatch the passing moment and examine it for signs of eternity is the noblest of occupations. It is Olympian. Therefore I undertook to be monitor of the Washington seasons, when the government was not looking. Though it was only for my own good, that is how the poorest of us may benefit the world. A more ambitious man might seek to improve the President of the United States.

The city of Washington is not so well established a fact as 38° 53′ North, 77° 2′ West, which came first. The setting preceded the city and will survive it. Before public buildings were erected here to house files and file clerks, our reddish-brown fellow men were doubtless accustomed to observing how the revolution of the seasons manifested itself at the fall line of the Potomac River. To improve my education, I wished to familiarize myself with what they had observed *sub specie aeternitatis*. If I could learn just when spring arrived, in what manner and in what guises, I should have grown in knowledge of reality and established a bond of common experience with my fellow travelers in eternity. My monitoring of the seasons in off hours would thus be more substantial and altogether a more serious matter than anything I could do for the government. I had not had compunctions at interrupting the dictation of an official document to observe, from a government window, a flight of swans moving south overhead; and while I have now forgotten what the official paper was about, I remember the swans. They made me an honorary brother of Audubon then and there, enlarging my experience to include life on the western frontier a century and a half ago.

Another year I shall, perhaps, insert advertisements in the newspapers after New Year's Day, calling attention to the forthcoming arrival of spring in town, proclaiming it the most lavish spectacle on earth, and offering hilltop or valley-bottom seats at a stiff price. You will see how the people flock to buy tickets, though they never thought it worth a free view before. One would like, however, to be honest and announce over the radio to all men: The spring shall make you free, the price of wolfram will enslave you.

The city of Washington has never had the praise it deserves from those of us who do not give ourselves altogether to city life. Unlike New York, it makes room for nature in its midst and seems to welcome it. There is Rock Creek Park, with its forests and fields, which

wanders through Washington and remains uncor-
rupted. The city passes over Rock Creek Valley on
bridges a hundred and twenty-five feet above and
heeds it not. The muskrat swims and raises its young
in the woodland stream beneath Connecticut Avenue,
never knowing of the crowded buses and taxis that
swarm overhead. Peering down from the railing of the
bridge, you overlook what might be a virgin forest
with an undiscovered and half-hidden river wandering through it. You may see a hawk circling over
the trees, or a kingfisher following the stream. This is
as the birds view the world when they fly in their migrations over the forests of the Northwest or the un-
trodden jungles of Central America. Especially after
a cold night in fall, the warm sun rises over a dawn
mist curled like a dragon through the length of the
valley below. Once in early October, when all else
was silent and the first rays of the sun shone from the
horizon over the still shrouded valley, from far below
the mist came the repeated call of the Carolina wren,
kirtleyou, kirtleyou, kirtleyou, kirtleyou . . . I could
build a house on the bridge and live happily there forever, turning my back to the street. At either end, the
valley slopes rise steeply to its level so that, from the
railing, you look directly into the top of the forest—its
maze of branch and foliage, its leafy green chambers
and recesses, the ground far below—and see it from
the inside like a bird perched in its upper stories. I
should prefer to think that the government built this
lofty bridge for a lookout, and that it bears traffic incidentally.

Elsewhere in Washington, parks, patches of forest,
and trees are common. Squirrels and rabbits can move
about a great part of the city at will. Bobwhites are at
home in it, and foxes may be found. The roosting ground of the turkey vultures some two and a half

miles up Rock Creek, reported by John Burroughs in 1861, is still used by them, though the city has overtaken it. In the late afternoon you may see half a hundred vultures circling over the Kennedy-Warren Hotel, which now dominates the site, or perched on its roof. Tenants of fashionable apartment houses complain that they are kept awake at night by the hooting of barred owls.

I go from my apartment, in the midst of the city, to the countryside of Virginia and Maryland entirely by ways that lead through woods and open green spaces. It is cross-country to Tierra del Fuego or Alaska. From my doorstep through the park to the mouth of Rock Creek, where it empties into the river, is no more than ten minutes by bicycle. Beyond, only a margin of greensward separates the road from the embankment. Across the river the wooded shore of Anolastan Island might in its summer foliage be the forested bank of a tropical river. All through the early spring, after the ice goes out, American mergansers, the drakes showing as sparkles of white at that distance, swim and dive in close to its shore or sun themselves on fallen trees. In summer white egrets hunt there. Once I saw through my binoculars a native, naked except about the loins, hunting with spear or gun along its shore. He vanished into the shrubbery as I watched, and I have never seen any other sign of human habitation on the island.

Anolastan Island (now renamed Theodore Roosevelt Island) stands at the fall line of the Potomac, washed by fresh water above, by tidewater below. The ancient city of Georgetown, long ago incorporated into the city of Washington, confronts it on the left bank, having marked the limit of navigation to generations of river boatmen. Above, the river runs in cataracts between steep banks and through tortuous ways from the Alleghenies. At the head of Anolastan Island its turbulence ends abruptly. Below, it broadens and ceases to flow except with the gentle alternations of the tide. Its expanse bears twinkling sailboats and an occasional river steamer. Colonial mansions, Mount Vernon among them, overlook it; but there are also extensive tidal marshes and marshy inlets. A hundred miles beyond is Chesapeake Bay, and at last the great ocean itself. Washington thus stands at the innermost limit of the coastal plain, mediating between the coast and the interior. This has been forgotten now by those who live in the city, but it was well known at one time, when the river boats discharged their cargo at Georgetown for shipment by canal barge into the Northwest Territories, and loaded in turn the cargo brought down by the barges from the wild interior. It is still known to the red-breasted mergansers, which range upriver as far as Washington and put in at the Tidal Basin under the Jefferson Memorial, but stop here because it is the limit of their salt-water habitat, let other ducks go as far as they please. I do not know how the fishes regard the matter, but many of them doubtless hold like views, recognizing Washington as the frontier town it is.

In spring one faces south, which means one looks directly downriver from Washington. The Arlington Memorial Bridge forms a granite suture between North and South, connecting President Lincoln's Memorial in Washington with General Lee's Memorial in Arlington County. At the Arlington end it opens on grassy fields that, in season, accommodate horned larks, killdeer, and meadowlarks. The highway runs down the right bank past the Navy and Marine Memorial (bronze gulls scudding over a bronze wave), past the Highway Bridge, and past Roaches Run. Roaches Run is a marshy lagoon trapped between the National Airport, on one side, and the rail-

way tracks on the other. Ducks and gulls and herons
have remained faithful to it, despite low-roaring air-
planes and smoke-breathing locomotives. They are
accustomed to these dragons and these pterodactyls,
regarding them not. The government pays conscience
money here, posting the lagoon as a sanctuary and
scattering grain, like Ceres herself, for the wildfowl.
At the airport giant transports and little pursuit
planes squat in rows like somnolent dragonflies. The

killdeer share the field with them. At the southern end
of the airport, where a trickle of water from Arlington
County forms a wide marshy mouth as it empties into
the river, you look directly down on acres of open
water and marsh grass. This, the mouth of Four Mile
Run, is beloved by a variety of river birds and marsh
birds. I take it that the fattest frogs and most succulent
waterweeds are found here, amid the talus of steel
drums and other jetsam that has tumbled from the
brink of the airfield above.

From the airport to the outskirts of Alexandria, a
distance of a mile and a half, the age of smoke and
machinery has blackened the land. However, even
such a scene as this has moments when it becomes a

wonder. The morning of Easter Sunday, I was on my bicycle at six o'clock under a waning moon. It was dawn at seven, when I passed the airport. All along the Virginia shore locomotives were belching black smoke that flattened out on the west wind, at a low elevation, and was carried in rivers and lakes eastward, blotting out the sky from Roaches Run through Alexandria. In this cold dawn made sinister by artificial twilight, the locomotives were hooting at each other with authority or impatience or stubborn

anger, each an individual, each a life, so that for the moment it was not possible to escape the conviction that these hootings expressed great animal emotions, untamed, and were not mechanical. It was Gulliver's world.

The railway yards and the highway have been constructed over marshes that persist, but ink has replaced the marsh water and the reeds have turned black. It is still a paradise, however, for blackbirds, for a red-tailed hawk in winter, and along its fresher margins where the river washes it, for itinerant egrets of the late summer.

Beyond Alexandria for twelve miles the George Washington Memorial Highway follows the river to Mount Vernon through a setting of forest, river marshes, and open uplands. This, again, is fresh earth and fresh sky. Look up when you reach Washington's home at Mount Vernon and, like as not, you will see one or several American eagles soaring against the blue. They do duty for bronze eagles over Washington's tomb. In winter you may see them sitting hunched on the ice away out in the river, disdaining the passing gulls. Eagles are not uncommon anywhere along the Potomac, but their center of abundance is here in the bays and marshy inlets about Mount Vernon. To them, I have no doubt, the city of Washington is a sort of campground above the mouth of the Anacostia, erected yesterday by a wandering tribe of men, to be abandoned in due course. In the scope of an eagle's vision, it represents only a tiny usurpation of his immemorial domain, like an anthill by the front door or a hornet's nest under the eaves.

All winter long the world lies encased in its hard sheath. Frost is fastened upon the earth, the trees are brittle shells, the river acquires a plating of ice. Men likewise button themselves up in thick clothing, hiding limbs and torso. Woodchucks and chipmunks make their own graves and lie in them. Everything takes on an outward petrifaction, the earth and its creatures each dwelling in its own coffin. You cannot touch life anywhere, only its casing. This is a time for theory and hypocrisy, for imagined sin and affected virtue among men, a time to find fault in words and to reform the world on paper, a time for cleverness and scholarship, a time for vanity. Man makes himself at home on the earth like a flea in the ear of a sleeping dog, ordering matters to suit himself. Then spring comes, the casing melts off, and the living body of the earth is exposed to the sky for anyone to see and touch. Life slowly flushes and fills it.

The mathematicians reckon that spring begins March 21, but the mathematicians are a month behind the season the year around. For those who observe the first signs, spring comes earlier than others know. Before the end of January, while the scenery remains desolate and the sun leaves no warmth, the first sparks are already being enkindled in the breasts of songbirds. As I left my home at daybreak January 22, under a cloud rack becoming visible, in a dead tree across the street a cardinal was singing *cue-cue-cue-cue-cue-cue,* rapidly, all on one pitch and without variation. Up to that moment, for many silent months, I do not recall that my mind had been occupied with

other than the indoor thoughts of the hive. In its dark winter quarters it had survived entirely on a diet of paper: official documents provided by the government, supplemented by such reading as I had time for. The out-of-doors meant the weather, and the weather was a wintry nuisance with which one put up in those daily excursions to and from the office. One forgot about the seasons; the passage of time was measured by the unchanging flow and accumulation of paper; eternity was a pension in the future. Then the cardinal sang, waking me up, or at least penetrating and disturbing my sleep. Like the ground hog emerging

from his burrow, I blinked at the sky through the opening and snuffed the wind. It was still winter, except for the cardinal who had his own inner stirrings.

On the 28th, a Sunday, the temperature rose to freezing and the sun shone all morning through such a delicate haze as softens the horizons of spring. The same cardinal at daybreak, from the same tree, was singing *toowee toowee toowee toowee toowee,* then again *cue-cue-cue-cue-cue-cue.* The time for monitoring the arrival of spring was manifestly at hand, and I set off by bicycle to do so.

The river, when I came to it, was mainly frozen, but a few scattered flocks of gulls were busy about black openings in the ice. From the shrubbery close by the statue of William Jennings Bryan a white-throated sparrow unexpectedly sang the slow, high notes of his song, sweet and languid. Having finished, he did not repeat the performance, perhaps, for a week. On the other side of Memorial Bridge you could smell spring in the air, never so intoxicating as in this first whiff of the year. I unbuttoned my coat to it. I should say that I began unbuttoning my soul or inner man for the

first time in an age of months. On my left hand was
the river, bordered by a line of leaning poplars and
willows with shrubbery about their feet. On my right,
the sward that would again be green was sodden
where the warm sun thawed it. By the memorial of
flying gulls done in bronze, a cardinal and a song sparrow sang. The cardinal was repeating his full spring
song, two musical syllables going downstairs into the
cellar. The song sparrow tried the first few notes of his
own song, experimentally, but never got beyond them.
He reminded me how early it still was for spring. A
red-tailed hawk, sitting heavily in a tree by the river,
was still in winter quarters. At Roaches Run the open
water was crowded with wintering pintails chiefly, plus
a few black ducks, a few mallards, and four coots. Out
on the river opposite, some mergansers, red-breasted
and American, were swimming and diving in a wide-
open seam of the ice. By this time the haze had become cloud and overcome the sun. I buttoned up my
coat against the chilling air, thinking: it's going to
snow.

_____

To me the bicycle is in many ways a more satisfactory
invention than the automobile. It is consonant with
the independence of man because it works under his
own power entirely. There is no combustion of some
petroleum product from Venezuela to set the pedals
going. Purely mechanical instruments like watches
and bicycles are to be preferred to engines that
depend on the purchase of power from foreign
sources. You can be more independent, and therefore
more of a man, in a sailing vessel than in a power-
driven boat. In the former you can still keep going if
the national or international economy breaks down.
You need not trouble yourself about legislative enact-

ments for the exchange of goods and services, about international treaty arrangements for which your life is hostage. The price of power, on the other hand, is enslavement.

Bicycling, furthermore, is the nearest approximation I know to the flight of birds. The airplane simply carries a man on its back like an obedient Pegasus; it gives him no wings of his own. There are movements on a bicycle corresponding to almost all the variations in the flight of the larger birds. Plunging free downhill is like a hawk stooping. On the level stretches you may pedal with a steady rhythm like a heron flapping; or you may, like an accipitrine hawk, alternate rapid pedaling with gliding. If you want to test the force and direction of the wind, there is no better way than to circle, banked inward, like a turkey vulture. When you have the wind against you, headway is best made by yawing or wavering, like a crow flying upwind. I have climbed a steep hill by circling or spiraling, rising each time on the upturn with the momentum of the downturn, like any soaring bird. I have shot in and out through stalled traffic like a goshawk through the woods. The best way to ride, especially downhill, is with both hands in your pockets and leaning backwards. This is not so hard as it looks; like a bird, you control your direction perfectly by unconscious shifts in your balance. Especially on the long downslopes, this is to know the freedom of the wind. The air rushing past your ears reminds you that the birds must be partially deafened by their own speed.

Because you move under your own power, bicycling is to be compared rather to walking than to automobiling. By this standard, the ease and speed with which you encompass great distances seem miraculous. In an hour on the way to work I have covered ten or twelve miles, gone clean out of the city to look for signs of spring and come back into it untired and, in fact, refreshed for the day's work. In four or five hours of a Sunday I have covered fifty miles, visiting strange lands in Virginia or Maryland.

―――――――――

Though the Lord created the world in seven days, its annual re-creation takes longer. In the week following January 28, the temperature remained in the teens. The next Sunday, February 4, a light breeze came from the south and again the morning sun shone through a haze—until midday. The afternoon brought rain, sleet, and hail from a darkened sky. My friend Og and I bicycled south, down the river to meet the spring. This was not altogether quixotic, for there were birds wintering at Mount Vernon that would not arrive in Washington until the spring migration brought them: towhees, red-bellied woodpeckers, and field sparrows. They were toeing the mark. In the blackened marshes between the airport

and Alexandria, a flock of red-winged blackbirds were clearing their pipes but not yet singing. A flock of female redwings, not even clucking, landed in a tree by Roaches Run. At one point a song sparrow sang lustily. The forty-one species of birds that we counted that day, however, represented the wintering population, the base of departure from which we might measure the expected change of season.

At dawn the next day the pavements were glazed with frozen rain under low, solid clouds, but two or three cardinals sang tentatively and, for the first time this year, I heard a titmouse tirelessly calling *Peter, Peter, Peter. . . .* Two days later, though the hoarfrost was on the ground, the Carolina chickadees were singing their own spring song, that jaunty, complicated version of the blackcap's "phoebe" song: *dee-didee dee doo doo.* February 9, the weather turned mild and the sun melted most of the ice off the river. February 10 was balmy; a wind came from the south in occasional puffs, raising the temperature by evening to 59°. Not only song sparrows, titmice, chickadees, and cardinals sang now: the nuthatches were laughing vociferously, this being their own version of

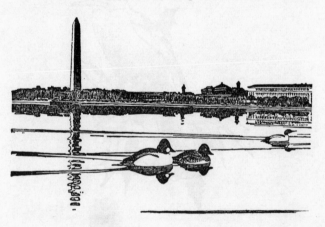

a spring song, and throughout the midday a mocking-bird sat in a holly tree outside the Department of the Interior and improvised. When Sunday came round again, February 11, it seemed inconceivable, looking out over the sunlit and rippling expanse of the river below Alexandria, that it could ever have been frozen.

When the ice goes out of the river and out of the marshes, the ducks and the gulls come in. This Sunday there must have been fewer American mergansers in the lower reaches of the Potomac and in Chesapeake Bay than a week before, because they had suddenly become abundant from Washington to Mount Vernon, in loose congregations of thirty or forty. The sun shone beneficently and the light west wind was just enough to stir the surface of the river. The elegant mergansers, seen through binoculars, rode the ripples serenely, the drakes sparkling white in the sun. The females seemed more real because less ornamental. The drake's head and neck at any distance might be carved out of wood and enameled black; but the smaller gray-and-brown female shows her alert eye, her toothed bill, and the feathers of her crest standing out in tufts behind. They swim about, parading and preening on the river, till suddenly, one after another, they vanish, leaving the surface empty except, per-

haps, for widening ripples. A moment later, one after another, they all bob up again to resume their preening and parading.

At the mouth of Four Mile Run, in addition to the pintails, black ducks, mallards, and mergansers we had seen along the river the week before, a flotilla of twenty-six scaup had come to anchor in this roadstead, and by the edge of the grasses a drake baldpate was keeping company with the pintails. These were, in their way, signs of spring. The redwings were tuning up in Potomac Yards this week as the week before, and elsewhere a Carolina wren sang abruptly from cover. Over the tidal marshes of Dyke, below Alexandria, a marsh hawk in the dark, immature plumage was quartering. Perhaps it should be accounted a new arrival.

The week that followed continued balmy, but winter returned with the weekend. Snow all day Saturday and a freezing west wind on Sunday. Og reported an Iceland gull, bird of the arctic never before recorded in Washington, just above the Memorial Bridge; and together we observed a pair of goldeneyes, those companions of winter, with a flock of half a hundred mergansers in the Tidal Basin. So early in the year, it takes a long view and a stubborn faith to recognize the advent of spring. Yet this is what it takes to recognize life itself and to embark upon it as an enterprise. It is the formula that, if I were a fairy godmother, I should bestow on my first godchild.

The next week was one of freezing weather followed by intermittent rains and steaming mists, followed in turn by a fine sunset, a fine sunrise, and October weather. By now the cardinals, song sparrows, and titmice were singing every morning, the cardinals beginning almost at the first hint of light, the sparrows not until the fact of day had been established, the titmice last of all. Perhaps it was equally a sign of the imminence of spring that this

week I began regularly to bicycle to work at daybreak by way of the Virginia shore. My route led
down Rock Creek, across the Memorial Bridge to
Roaches Run, back over the Highway Bridge, and
once around the Tidal Basin. The Tidal Basin is the
ornamental lagoon with stone embankments that
serves as a reflecting pool for the Jefferson Memorial
and, more distantly, the Washington Monument. It
provides a setting for the best-known ornament of the
Washington spring, the Japanese cherry trees on its
banks. It is not a wild pool in the wilderness, but
ducks, grebes, and loons consider it such. It has its
own characteristic wildlife. This week, as in the weeks
to come, the mergansers were scattered all over its surface amid the herring gulls.

———————

Matters had now advanced to the stage when you
could be reasonably sure that spring would arrive
with the first south wind. I take the advent of the first
migrating birds from the south as the final indication
of the opening of the spring season. As a personal matter I might set the date earlier by a month, for the
first spring thoughts are as good a token as any. They
accompany the first bird music and the first sunshiny
haze of the year. The equinox brings only the mathe-
matician's spring, and by that time, although he does
not know it, spring is half over. Just as the earliest fall
migrants flying south are said sometimes to pass the
latest spring migrants flying north, so my summer
thoughts are current with his intimations of spring. If
I wake up earlier next year, perhaps I shall find signs
of spring before New Year's Day, though I have to look
inward for them. In sheltered places the skunk cab-
bage makes a start in November, and so it might be
with spring thinking. The farmer regards the seasons

as two, summer and winter, with subseasons of transition; for spring and fall are not static, as summer and winter tend to be. To the naturalist who observes the flight of birds, however, the two seasons are spring and fall, with pauses between as when the piston hesitates at the bottom and at the top of its stroke. In Washington spring ends finally sometime in June, when the last blackpoll warbler takes its departure for the north, and fall begins the middle of July with the swarming of martins every evening to their roost at Pennsylvania Avenue and 7th Street, N.W., preparatory to flying south.

Sunday, February 25, the wind had gone around to the south and the sun shone through a haze. The first arrival of the year was a robin that flew over Rock Creek in the morning. On the uplands of Wellington, halfway between Alexandria and Mount Vernon, we came on the first flock of grackles, sauntering in black-and-purple elegance along the grass borders, perched on spires of cedar, or dragging their tails in labored flight. Their grating voices, all conversing together, were the voices of spring. Mourning doves, of which a scattered few had wintered, were suddenly common today. This was spring itself in its debut. These were the first arrivals of the first wave of migration. More came during the day, for on our return from Mount Vernon we found flocks of grackles where none had been in the morning and from Dyke to Washington the countryside was suddenly overrun with red-winged blackbirds. Against the reddening sky of evening, the blackbirds were flying, flock after flock, to roost in the big marshes.

Every morning now is a fresh wonder, no two quite the same. Thursday, March 1, a cloudless day, the west wind blowing easily across the city. By the time the sun rises now, about a quarter to eight, I am likely to be across the bridge and into Virginia, having myself arisen in the starlight. On a morning like this I have knotted a woolen scarf about my neck and tucked it into my jacket, for it is frosty and clear and the wind cuts. Looking across the river, I see the sun rise brilliantly between the silhouettes of the Monument and the Capitol dome, and feel its warm rays flash across the land at the same moment that the countryside about me is transformed into light and shadow. The trees at Roaches Run and the marsh grasses stand in relief, flooded by radiance from the horizon. All the birds are sparkling and ebullient in the sharp dawn. A redwing at the top of a tree is singing *conqueree-ee-ee,* shaking out his black-and-scarlet wings and spreading his tail at each utterance. Three grackles are clucking and grating to one another in the thicket. This is life beginning all over again, emerging from the darkness and damp into the new day. It is spring in microcosm. The tide is out, and where an area of marsh grass is exposed in the middle of the lagoon a great blue heron stands motionless. Another comes in from behind the island like a drifting feather, the sun illuminating it from below, drops its legs, uncurls its neck, and alights silently near the first. A horned grebe sits by its solitary self across the water. Two coots swim about the edge of the grasses, pumping their heads. I have already formed a nodding acquaintance with them.

On one side of the wooded island that is almost connected with the near shore, right up to the bank at my feet, the water is crowded with pintails beyond counting. Some sit on floating logs preening, others swim about in groups, holding their heads high on their curved stems to view me. Perhaps they think me a sign of spring, with my binoculars, as indeed I am.

A few in closest to shore take alarm, leap from the surface, and flap out to put down with little splashes among their fellows beyond. Mixed in with them, or preening along the shore of the island, are big black ducks and a few mallards. Farther out, in open water, is a flock of American mergansers. This completes the picture except for a score of herring gulls, some wailing mournfully. One gull, with a prize in its bill, flies zigzag, dodging to escape a rabble of suitors at its tail. When it finally drops the prize another picks it up and the chase continues, like boys playing tag in the freshness of morning. Occasionally there is a great outburst of wailing and screaming among them.

Before dawn on Saturday, after a night of heavy rain, I went out into a saturated world, no stars showing. The wind was from the south, as warm as buttered toast, heavy and smelling of rain. Coasting down the dark, glistening road through the park, I

caught the wild odor of the tidal marshes downriver, a smell of the ocean itself, of fish, of decaying vegetation and pungent marsh ooze, of wilderness. Near the Tidal Basin a robin was caroling, the first heard this year though they had been seen every day since Sunday. The fish crows appeared to have increased along the waterfront at Potomac Park in the gray dawn. Less strident in their calls than the common crows which inhabit the wooded and upland parts of Washington, they perched among the damp trees of the embankment in little groups, conversing softly and continuously like old men.

Anyone could have recognized by Sunday, March 4, that spring was here, for the golden forsythia was suddenly in bloom along the Mount Vernon highway, and the lily of the valley in flower at the edge of the woods. It must have happened overnight, under the warm rain and the south wind. The woods and fields still stood in penciled outline, the trees mere skeletons

against the sky, but the first touches of color that would at last fill the entire landscape had been applied. Half a dozen wood ducks had arrived at the Dyke marshes, and green-winged teal at Dyke and Four Mile Run. Four black vultures, ponderous and somber, circled over Mount Vernon, supplementing the eagles and turkey vultures that drifted across the sky. Down the wooded path bordering the marshes at Dyke we drove the first woodcock of the year, flushing it repeatedly. It would alight beyond the first bend in the path and wait for us to come up with it again, aberrant bird with misplaced eyes and disproportioned bill, waddling on uncertain feet, alert for flight. Then, with an explosive whistling of wings, flying jaggedly in a series of impulses, it would disappear around the next bend.

Below Mount Vernon on the wooded river shore, the first phoebe of the year, and it was only March 4. A migrating winter wren, a fox sparrow, and the first meadowlark singing. It was a month to the day since our first excursion downriver, and of the fifty-two species of birds that we counted ten were listed for the first time. Grackles, redwings, robins, and doves were now common to abundant everywhere.

In full sunlight, where the highway ran through deciduous woods on either hand, some strange bird with glowing wings or a great golden moth was weaving and circling, fluttering silently out over the highway, silently into the woods, back over the highway again. O beautiful, on wings through which the sun shines golden! Surely there never was such a creature alive! But it came close, fluttering and flittering in and out between us, and up close we saw what it was: a tawny-colored bat. Off into the woods at last, fluttering and dipping still, till we saw it no more.

A scientist later identified the apparition for me by my description as the red bat, *Lasiurus borealis;*

but with half a mind I was still disposed to believe we
had seen—who knows what?

————————

The multitudes of gulls that appear in Washington
with the spring attract the attention of government
workers, as well as students of nature, by their numbers. When the lawns are soggy with rain they assem-

ble in their hundreds on the grounds about the
Washington Monument and the Lincoln Memorial,
and on the Ellipse before the White House, marching
over the sod with uncertain dignity. Apparently they
feed on worms forced to the surface to escape drown-
ing. Overhead, gleaming white against the storm
clouds, they mill in large whorls, mingling their thin
cries with those of their fellows on the ground.

Individual birds, or several at a time, detach themselves from the swarm above, parachuting from the
sky on arched wings, and, upon alighting, run two or
three breathless steps before they catch their pedes-
trian balance and dignity. They scatter before you as
you walk toward them, the more timid taxiing away
across the common, beating their wings to regain the
freedom of the sky. These are mainly ring-billed gulls,
though you will see herring gulls, larger than the rest,
scattered among them.

Of all the gulls on our eastern seaboard, large and
small, the ringbill seems to me to represent the opti-
mum size for efficient gull-flight; for gull-flight is *sui*

generis, distinct from the flight of all other fowl. Gulls are not like shearwaters and albatrosses, gliders that skim stiffly over the waves on fixed wings. Neither are they like the great soaring birds, the eagles and vultures, that spread their wings and rest indefinitely upon the air currents. The feature of gull-flight is flexibility of wing, aerial deftness, the capacity for a thousand slight, continuous adjustments of wing and tail to the air in which they move. The great black-backed and herring gulls sacrifice some of this deftness to their size and weight, though they may gain in easy soaring. Where the wind does not assist them, their flight is labored. The little Bonaparte's gulls, on

the other hand, and to a lesser extent the laughing gulls, are quickness and grace itself, but because they lack the momentum of heavier birds they must be more continuously flapping and flicking their wings to sustain themselves. The middle-sized ringbill is just right, illustrating gull-flight in its perfection. Among the laboring herring gulls you see the myriad ringbills darting and weaving over the river, one sweeping past in a slanted arc from the sky to the surface or from the surface to the sky, another rising straight up like a feather, falling off on one wing, backing, dropping, zooming, and away again without effort.

Tuesday at dawn, rolling black clouds cover the sky, a warm, wet wind with a touch of wildness in it is whipping up the river. From the mouth of Rock Creek to the Memorial Bridge a blizzard of ring-billed gulls is raging, the white birds hanging in the wind or sweeping down it against a black sky. You know them from the herring gulls, of which there are a few among them, by their thin, high cry with its rasping quality. They have none of the varied, melodious, and mournful notes that are the herring gull's principal distinction. The air here is full of the ringbill cry as the sky is full of their forms. It is a wonder that, sweeping and darting and hovering in their turbulent multitudes, as far as you can see, they do not collide with one another. The wind in which they swirl so easily is like a solid obstruction to the bicyclist straining to make headway against it.

The Tidal Basin, as usual, is swarming with herring gulls, crying in the wind, with never a ringbill among them. At Roaches Run it is the same. I judge that the herring gulls prefer the lagoons and estuaries to the open flowing water where the ringbills congregate. The particular preference of the ringbills is for the waters off the mouths of streams that empty into the river, and there you see them in their greatest number—whether it is the mouth of Rock Creek or of the Anacostia River.

Wednesday is still warm, though now the same wild wind has veered to the west. Dark blankets of cloud are still moving overhead. For the first time I kept to the left bank of the river, past Memorial Bridge and Highway Bridge. Beyond is all open going for two miles to Hains Point, cycling along the embankment as at the edge of the sea, separated from the river only by a railing of pipes. On the left is the flat or gently rolling lawn of East Potomac Park, supporting isolated trees, which extends to the other side of the peninsula (for that is what this is), where it fronts on Washington Channel and, across it, the docks and fish markets of the city. At the Point, facing the mouth of the Anacostia, a thousand or more ring-billed gulls take off from the turf as I sweep around it, filling the air with white flakes against the dark clouds. I set down the increase in gulls, since the days when scattered flocks could be found playing about openings in the ice, as another sign of spring.

It is curious how the preoccupations of the hive fill us, driving out all memory of the universe into which we were born. Perhaps the whole human race may be said to suffer from amnesia, not knowing whence it came or why it finds itself here. But we inhabitants of the hive suffer from double amnesia, one case within another, and are removed one stage further from the ultimate reality in which we have our beginning and our end. We have forgotten that we live in the universe, and that our civilization itself is merely an elaboration of the palm-leaf hat that one of our ancestors tried on ten thousand years ago to ward off the sun, a more complicated and ample version that now not only wards off the sun but shuts out the view. We have lost ourselves within it. Yet some have told me, when I set out to have a look at the stars or to watch the migration of birds, that I was escaping reality! I judge that it is they who are escaping into the artificial problems of their workaday life. The tailor makes himself a prisoner in his own shop, and if you speak to him of other dimensions than those he knows in his trade he will not sleep nights. "To an amazing degree people's environment has come to consist of machines and man-made things, much as the environment of animals is made up of natural objects and growing things." I quote from the findings of the Harvard Committee appointed to study the problem of *General Education in a Free Society*, and which reported on the increasing difficulty of educating men for the universe.

I have looked through the Washington newspapers in season without finding any account of the arrival of ducks or the visitations of gulls, although they re-

ported the visit of a French functionary and the return from her wintering grounds in the south of somebody's wife. It was all news of the hive, with not a word of events in the outside world. The magazines for sale on the stands and the new books displayed in the shops reflect this preoccupation. Our civilization, apparently, has become divorced from the universe and is feeding on itself.

This is equally apparent when you listen to our talk. Our society is made up of workers, not men. We are obsessed with the inadequacies of the hive, which does not support us to our satisfaction, and attribute these inadequacies to the shortcomings of our fellow workers. We are possessed by a sort of panic at finding ourselves dependent on one another. We are tormented by the fear of what might happen to us if our fellow workers should be negligent or ill-willed or simply too smart for us. Consequently, we clamor all together for a new ordering of matters, for new rules and new regulations and new restraints to secure us

against one another. We find ourselves fettered by the chains we have designed for our fellows, and threatened with destruction by the weapons we have invented to destroy them; yet we do not, on that account, cease our frantic search for more binding fetters and more terrible engines of destruction.

Under the circumstances it is proper to wonder why our entrapped multitudes do not seek escape from the hive, once more asserting their individual independence as men. The door stands open on the outside world. I conclude that we have lost our knowledge of the outside world, and fear of the unknown is greater than that of any accustomed horror. I have seen a bird cowering in its cage when the door was opened for its escape.

You will find that any reference to the times when we men were not altogether dependent on our hive organization arouses a general revulsion among us. It appears that before our swarm took refuge in the hive it lived in darkness, that the only light shining in the world is the artificial light of the hive. Obsessed with fear at our dependence on one another, we are even more fearful of being dependent once more on ourselves. It is the nature of slavery to render its victims so abject that at last, fearing to be free, they multiply their own chains. You can liberate a freeman, but you cannot liberate a slave.

It follows that the training of a worker for the hive is something distinct from the education of a freeman for the universe. The purpose of education in a free society of men is to gain knowledge of the universe in which they live and their relation to it. To realize our independence we must know what we can about ourselves and about our outer environment. The laws of the universe are more important than the law of society, the limits that it puts to man's action are the limits that count. Man learns to know the universe, and his place in it, from the accumulated experience and study of mankind, corroborated by his own observation. But the worker who has retreated into the hive can dispense with knowledge of it; all he needs is to master one of the technical skills required by the society. In return for performing one operation, the hive will feed him and shelter him for the duration of his life, and lay him away when he dies. The coal miner, the radio operator, and the file clerk need not understand the nature of a cow to consume their allotments of bottled milk. Because, in reading the newspapers, books, and magazines, I see that the majority favor the elimination of useless education and the provision, in its place, of more thorough training in the skills, I come to the gloomy conclusion that most of us have abandoned all desire to be free. We shall continue to sell our birthright for what we take to be the security of the hive until we have destroyed ourselves and it. When that time comes, perhaps the remnant of us, thrown unwillingly on the resources of our own manhood, will be able to make a fresh start.

Meanwhile, it is not likely that the newspapers will carry news from outside.

It has been said before that a fundamental aim of education is to enable men to live in time and space beyond the present and the immediate. The majority of uneducated men and women appear to lead entirely somnambulistic lives, never pausing between the cradle and the grave to look up from the immediate task in hand, never raising their heads to take stock of the long past or to survey the plains and mountain ranges that surround them. In their trade, in their daily occupations, even in the thoughts they express and the opinions they hold, they move without consciousness of worlds beyond their own. Ask the uneducated tailor for a description of the universe and see if it does not bear a striking resemblance to his own shop, even though the reality stretches away from his door. To the uneducated politician the goal of life is the advancement of his party, to the uneducated intellectual it is the advancement of his cause or the acceptance of his dogma. Each measures the world by his own shadow, overlooking the assistance he has from the sun in casting it. All these people are the victims of circumstances they cannot hope to understand, whether it is the American mechanic who shouts for democracy or the European barber who shouts for a dictator. In their somnambulism they are bound to the wheel of the immediate present, and will be freed only when education has awakened them to the breadth and scope of the universe they share in common.

The discovery of spring each year, after the winter's hibernation, is like a rediscovery of the universe. In my bleak winter quarters, preoccupied with the problems of the moment, I had forgotten the immeasurable richness and continuance of life. This recollected smell of fresh loam in my nostrils is the smell of eternity iself.

Winter or summer, if you wish to match yourself against a wilderness, I can recommend nothing better locally than the tidal marshes around Dyke, a couple of miles below Alexandria. I daresay the open marsh here, excluding the swampy woods that extend up- and down-river from it, does not cover an area half so large as that of the airport, which is a mile and a half in its greatest length, but the difficulty of making your way through it gives it size enough. At low tide you may struggle step by step through marsh grasses that rise to your shoulder, sinking at every few steps above your knees into some unseen hole or into the smooth and treacherous ooze.

Only a determined man can make his way across these marshes. They are deceptive, for they hide the existence of innumerable water inlets until he stumbles upon them. Then he must work his way up their banks until, God willing and the tide remaining low, he finds them narrow enough to risk a leap, when he again sets forth to the next obstructing channel. These inlets penetrate the marsh everywhere, a network through which the tide flows in and out with the slow regularity of an animal breathing. We have tried a flat-bottomed boat too, pulling and pushing it at high tide through the inlets; but the ooze soon clings to its bottom and the reeds block its way. The man carries the boat more than the boat the man. Vultures, marsh hawks, and sometimes eagles sweep past like shadows, ducks whistle by like grapeshot, herons flap their great cambered wings and trail their legs over the grasses; but a man has to struggle like Laocoön for every yard gained.

It is so late in the season when the new grass appears in the marshes, after the woods are already in leaf, that its springing may almost be taken as a sign of summer. Although the elm trees had flowered this week all over Washington, and we had just had an April day in which sprinkles of warm rain swept through the sunlit city as from an accidentally diverted garden hose, the bleached and broken grasses of last year still covered the marshes on Sunday, March 11. The wind was in the west and the sun shone. Where an inlet passes under the highway, a mixed company of ducks burst up from the hummocks where they had been preening, when I stopped my bicycle, and swept out into the open marsh, black

ducks and mallards quacking, a female wood duck crying *oo-eek oo-eek oo-eek* . . .

Just beyond the inlet is as good a place as any to
enter the marsh. A path leads into the woods and becomes lost in swampy thickets choked with brambles.
I pushed my way through them, like the Prince coming to the rescue of the Sleeping Beauty, thinking
myself alone until an invisible orchestra struck up and
I was surrounded by ringing melody. It was the richest kind of bird music, coming in chorus from every
direction, but wholly unfamiliar to me. Then I saw
that the underbrush and brambles were full of fox
sparrows, all singing. After a minute or two they
stopped as abruptly as they had begun, and did not

resume for all my waiting. A dozen yards more brought me to the edge of the open marsh, into the sunlight once more.

For two hours I struggled through the marsh, filling the sky with ducks that took off from the inlets ahead of me, sometimes only two or three, sometimes fifteen or twenty at once. The quacking black ducks and mallards were heavy on the wing, circling in masses all about the horizon. Alongside them, the smaller baldpates, pintails, and wood ducks flew in swift, compact groups. They rose high in the air, circled, and came sweeping down in long curves over the reeds. They circled away again, exploring the whole marsh with its myriad veins, before they decided it was safe to put down and, on suddenly set wings, scudded all together over the grass-tops and disappeared into some inlet hidden from view. When they put into the smaller inlets, they backed their wings and dropped vertically from fifteen or twenty feet.

Several times I flushed ducks no larger than pigeons, the green-winged teal, swiftest of all, sweeping like sandpipers over the marshes, here and away again before you knew it.

I could never hope to stalk any of these surface-feeding ducks for a close view of them on the water, but the little groups of American mergansers on the two broadest inlets were not nearly so wary. I crept up to spy on their privacy from the rushes, until one of them would spy me. Then, croaking softly, they would all taxi along the inlet, splashing with wings and feet, at last rising from the water and, stretched taut, make off like arrows to the open river. On one inlet a horned grebe, when it saw me, sank down like a rock and did not reappear. On another, a coot pat-

tered away from me about the bend. A greater yellowlegs flew across the outer edge of the marshes on
its way north, far in advance of schedule according to
the bird calendar (although that evening I saw half a
dozen more migrating in a flock across the airport).
Though it was not a warm day, little companies of
gnats were to be seen about the wooded edges of the
marshland.

To complete the picture, you have not only singing
blackbirds and song sparrows to add: two eagles with
white heads and tails were beating back and forth or
soaring aloft; turkey vultures and a single female
marsh hawk were circling or sweeping by; a red-shoul-
dered hawk hung overhead; great blue herons trav-
ersed the grassy pastures with wings beating slowly
and easily, alighting on their long stalks by the borders of inlets, taking off again with the peculiar slow
buoyancy of their flight, as if they were not altogether
heavier than air. Crows struggled into the wind. Gulls
flapped past or circled out over the river. This abundance of life, virile and variegated, expanding over
the countryside with the change of season, was worth
an amphibious excursion from the highway.

You cannot go into the marshes without getting your
feet wet, and I am told that this is dangerous by
many who have never tried it. You cannot go out into
the world at all without exposing yourself to the
unconditioned air, and I may someday be told that
this too is dangerous. All these generations man has
been adapting himself to his natural environment,
and now he has discovered that in the hive, if he will
keep to it, he can adapt the environment to himself.
What began as a comfort ends as necessity. I have
a reasonably tough carapace that protects me from
wind and weather. I inherited it. But it may be that

my posterity will have to be kept in incubators and fed on predigested foods. The price of too much comfort is the loss of freedom. I had as soon become addicted to alcohol or opium as to the comforts of the hive, for one addiction is as unacceptable as another when it comes to paying for my independence. In any case, I never knew anyone who appreciated an indulgence to which he had become accustomed. Such persons simply suffer if they have to do without; they have sold their independence for nothing. Our descendants may achieve absolute comfort, at the cost of freedom, but they will not have the enjoyment of it. My solicitous friends who have never had wet feet cannot know what it is to have dry feet, though they put on rubbers to ward off the dew.

By retreating from the world and insulating ourselves against it we are achieving a security as spurious as our comforts are hollow. No need to bite the coin that is offered for our independence, since any coin is false that purchases what is beyond price. Those who give up their carapaces for the hive that shelters them will all perish in the first catastrophe. The first draft of outer air coming through the first breach will kill them. I had rather be strong in my own strength to resist disease than to give up my strength in the hope that civilization will protect me from exposure to it. I would rather be able to take my drinking water where I find it, like the fox or the Indian, than to give up any acquired immunity to the organisms it contains on the chance of being able forever to filter them out. Who is more secure, the Indian who drinks swamp water or those of us who have to have our processed water out of a bottle? The Indian is exposed to a thousand little risks every day, but I would not exchange them for the one big risk that we have taken with ourselves and our posterity. A lady I knew had a parrot she kept in a steam-heated apartment, covering its cage with flannel every night. She was at a loss to know how I could let my parrot climb among the trees in a snowstorm, when hers would be killed by a cool draft. She contented herself that her parrot was delicate (without asking why) and, to take no chances, heaped on an extra flannel at night. One night the flannels slipped off and next day the parrot was dead. God save me from such loving care and give me wet feet. God save me from those doctors who will rob me of my health to keep me well. I pity the little children of the rich in the city, seeing how the more delicate they become the more they are swathed in wool or encased in rubber to protect them from the elements. I had rather raise up one man to front the world than half a hundred dependents that dare not breathe the outside air. But you do not grow hardy plants in a hothouse.

————————————

Scholars of the Middle Ages recognized twelve winds, but I have studied the matter and, as regards my country, reduced their twelve to three: the northwest, the south, and the east. Along the upper part of the eastern seaboard, the northwest wind may blow from the north or from the west, but it is all one wind. It is the most powerful of our winds, bringing clear horizons and cold weather, sunny days and frosty, starlit nights. It is dominant in the fall, to the great advantage of migrating birds, and in winter. The south wind is the wind of spring and summer, a balmy wind with a gentle haze as its badge. It transports the spring migrants and enough moisture to bring out the verdure. The east wind has no season. It comes capriciously, remaining sometimes several days, bringing the fog and the steady rain from the Atlantic Ocean. You feel the east wind in your bones. In summer, however, it is infrequent, and most of the rainfall comes on evening thunderstorms out of the west. These three winds leave no room for any other, the northwest wind extending through ninety degrees from north to west, the south wind from west to south, and the east wind from east of south to east of north. Your "four winds" or your "twelve winds" are not found in these parts, and I suspect that they are, in fact, mythical or metaphysical abstractions.

Monday, March 12, the wind was heavy from the south and the day grew steadily warmer. Tuesday was clear, cloudless, and balmy, the wind from the west. Wednesday the wind rose again from the south, the haze and warmth returned. The south wind continued Thursday, the warmest day yet. It continued Friday, and by four o'clock the record temperature of 86° Fahrenheit had been set. It continued Saturday, when the temperature rose to 87°. Sensible men devested themselves, while those who read the calendar rather than the thermometer ran their fingers around inside their collars and sweated. Doors and windows were thrown open, and in the evening people coming out of hibernation congregated in little groups about the street entrances of their houses to discuss the weather. It was surprising to find what thronging life the city contained.

By the end of this week robins and mockingbirds were in full song all over the city. House sparrows and starlings were carrying bits of straw, the sparrows bedeviling one another noisily in the gutters. Flickers, red-bellied woodpeckers, and a phoebe appeared in the city. The pintails were departing for their nesting grounds in the Northwest, and by Friday, of all the dense flock that had wintered at Roaches Run, only two were left. The drake mergansers also went north to take up their summer quarters before the females should arrive. In January and February, the males and females had been present in equal numbers. By Tuesday of this week the proportion had changed to one in four. I counted twenty-four female American mergansers to only six drakes, and on the Tidal Basin a drake red-breasted merganser had four females in his train.

Another sign of the season: A drake American merganser on the Basin was swimming in tight circles about the dead body of a female floating on its side so that only an upturned section of its underparts showed above-water. After two minutes in which the male was obviously invoking the powers of life, he climbed onto the dead body and copulated with it, lifting the limp head in his bill. The mystical act accomplished, the female returned to life and swam off happily with her rescuer. I do not know whether Zeus, who was practiced in these matters, ever assumed the form of a merganser.

We may assume that Eve was formed from the rib of Adam, not by a gradual development but by a single act of creation. Athene, too, was fully grown and accoutered when she sprang in one bound from the head of Zeus. Aphrodite, who had herself risen whole from the sea, transformed the ivory statue into a living bride for Pygmalion on the instant, without any false starts or piecemeal additions. In the long perspective, viewing a span of days as but a moment, spring is likewise a sudden awakening. Thus the rhythm of creation may be quick or slow, depending on the observer's standpoint. In my view the flash of lightning creates a whole landscape and abolishes it instantaneously, while to some other creature it may dawn and fade like the day itself, and the length of the day exceed a lifetime. One can back off from events in time as from objects in space, thereby altering the perspective. The history of Methuselah, who lived nine hundred sixty and nine years, is written in a sentence, while the history of Napoleon, who died at fifty-two, occupies a library. Spring in my childhood came more quickly than it does today. The earth simply threw off its winter blanket and merged in its primal beauty, garlanded and sweet scented, accompanied by the dawn music of innumerable voices.

If you examine any development minutely, you bring it to a stop. The present is frozen, nothing *happens* in it. The high-speed camera, which records only the real and instantaneous present, proves that the charging locomotive is standing still, and the same revelation was once recorded on a Grecian urn.

> Ah, happy, happy boughs! that cannot shed
> Your leaves, nor ever bid the Spring adieu . . .

I may go to sleep at dusk beneath a bush and, waking in the morning, find that it has flowered overnight, but only the interval of darkness, which hides the bush from my scrutiny, makes this possible. If I could sit up all night watching, I should see nothing happen at all, and though it was in flower at dawn my preoccupation with the present would prevent my knowing that it had ever been otherwise. Some magician always puts us to sleep when the scene is about to change. Thus spring, however closely you watch for it, comes as a succession of surprises. You stand guard all day and see nothing; then overnight you find the bare trees have budded and a myriad new birds have arrived.

It was now almost two months since that bleak morning when the cardinal had reminded me that winter would not last forever, and now the forsythia was in bloom, the elms had flowered, along the river at dusk clouds of blackbirds traveled toward their roosting grounds in the big marshes, passing smaller clouds of starlings, coming the other way to roost in the city. It was no longer a matter of listening for an isolated cardinal or song sparrow at dawn; for now, at dawn and dusk alike, and at intervals during the day, the robins stationed in the treetops filled the atmosphere with their uninterrupted caroling, *cheer-up cheery cheer-up cheery cheerily cheer-up . . .*, and then the rapid succession of call notes as if the birds were near to bursting with their passionate vitality. The earth had been filling with music, mourning doves consoling themselves in solitary places, white-throats at the other end of the scale singing their equally slow and sad but ethereal songs, nuthatches barking or laughing at one another in the deep woods as they clung upside-down beneath branches or against the trunks, chickadees chattering softly or breaking into their high *dee-didee dee doo doo,* titmice inventing all sorts of surprising phrases now as a relief from their incessant *Peter, Peter, Peter . . .*, downy woodpeckers emitting their dwindling bursts of sound, the occasional mockingbird performing by himself as if to show the world that he could overmatch any one of these or all together. . . . In the marshes, still sere and gray, the blackbirds clucked and sang and the ducks had increased, while gulls swarmed in the river. . . .

With the unseasonable heat of the past few days, Act I was now complete. The stage was set, earlier than ever this year, for the main developments.

II

AFTER three days' absence from Washington I returned to find how much spring had advanced. Willows, barberry, and many shrubs, all of which had been bare, were in leaf. The shrub magnolias were in flower and, best of all, throughout most of the city the cherry trees had blossomed. That was Tuesday, March 20. Friday was the day of full glory for the Japanese cherry trees that line the Tidal Basin. This is a wonder by itself, worthy of a civic holiday. Indeed, the people of Washington make it a holiday to the best of their ability, coming to the Basin at midday in pilgrimage from all over the city. I was there first, however, visiting it at sunrise. The morning was not quite warm yet, though it promised a warm day: not a cloud in the sky and not a breath of wind. I bicycled along the embankment alone, through a world embowered, under canopied masses of white bloom. The scene was magical, as if reality had given way to an illusory kingdom of flower and light, the light shimmering and ghostlike in its reflection from the masses of bloom overhead. They seemed a distillation of light, without weight or substance. The landscape was arrayed as if the earth were having its own mystic wedding festival, all in white close up, nacreous white in the distance, across the mirror of still water. It was silent and motionless, like a vision too insubstantial to last beyond the moment. The reality above seemed no less a wonderful illusion than its reflection in the water below.

I went there again with a friend at midday under the heat of the sun. The banks and the lawns beneath the flowered trees were thronged with a happy multitude, clerks and stenographers, officials, soldiers,

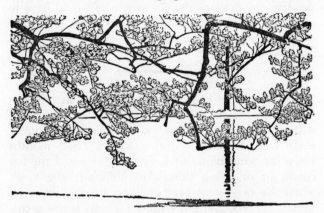

sailors, housewives, laughing, greeting one another, making holiday. Vendors were all about, selling ice cream and peanuts. Little boys kept their elders in a state of nervous anxiety, straying through the crowd, threatening to fall off the embankment, or clamoring for ice cream. Half the people had cameras and were striving for an opening in the crowd through which they could photograph the trees. For the inhabitants of Washington, this was the first unmistakable day of spring, an occasion for festivity. During the next few days, all over the city, everybody would ask everybody else whether he had been to see the cherry blossoms. Uncounted government stenographers, who had for a moment forgotten the ache and the emptiness, would now write home—to Austin, to Dubuque, to St. Louis, to Mudville, to Los Angeles—saying they had seen the cherry blossoms. Then the whole business would be forgotten for another year, the mirage gone, the workaday world of the city unchanged.

Two mornings later the freshness had already gone from the scene. Fallen blossoms were beginning to litter the ground, amid the litter of peanut bags, cardboard ice-cream containers, cigarette butts, and torn newspapers. Perhaps the old men who would have to clean up with their pointed sticks were glad that spring comes but once a year.

Most city people know the seashore only in summer, when the beaches are "bathing beaches," crowded with other city people at play. They know nothing of their true desolation, during the deserted months when the wind blows cold, when it rains and the fog comes in or flying snowflakes obliterate the view; when the occasional beachcomber, stirring up sandpipers, plovers, and gulls along his way, is too preoccupied with holding his own against the elements to pay attention to the rafts of ducks outside the surf and the flocks of them beating over the foam, or to the solitary loon flying low through the shifting valleys of the ocean. In a like sense, I doubt that most Washingtonians, who relax there on Sunday, would recognize East Potomac Park as I know it. To me, the solitary beachcomber of the early morning, it is like the beaches in winter, vast and lonely. One emerges from the city into an expanded view in which the sky dominates. The wind is visible, for it raises a chop in the river and whips the willow branches along two miles of curving embankment to Hains Point. It is tangible and fights me foot by foot along the riverside to the Point, then blows me down the channelside like a leaf in a gale. I have run before it, covering two miles in what seemed a breath-taking moment, simply by holding the wings of my coat out with each hand to catch the force of it. I shall make a bicycle sail, one day, and invent a new sport.

On calm hazy mornings the river is like dark glass, the air or water currents made visible by irregular lines of floating soot and jetsam drawn over it. Far away across the water, under that immensity of sky, I see the Virginia shore, the grove of trees that hides Roaches Run, the smudged horizon over the railway yards and Alexandria, and the airport where the silver planes glistening afar appear to be drying off their wings in the rising sun. When the tide is high the river spills over the embankment, and toward the Point I find myself splashing through water, riding my bicycle through the river. On the inside is rolling lawn with a few windswept trees. A thin grove of bald cypress has been planted at the Point. They are not here as in the cypress swamps of the deep South, where they grow shaggy and immense with age, but most delicate and stately, their tapered trunks having an aesthetic perfection like the columns of the Erechtheum. This bald cypress, which has been planted about the city and has attained a respectable size in Lafayette Park opposite the White House, is in many ways, the most beautiful tree in Washington.

No doctor ever prescribed a view of the open world for me, though it was the tonic I needed, rather than something to take in a glass before meals. Melville's Ishmael discovered the same cure. He took to the sea, that being his way "of driving off the spleen and regulating the circulation." It becomes necessary, occasionally, simply to throw open the hatches and ventilate one's psyche, or whatever you choose to call it. This means an excursion to some place where the sky is not simply what you see at the end of the street. Men were not born troglodytes, but they have become so even since Melville's day.

It is worth looking into this, since the doctors have failed to do so. I take it that the noblest trait of the human mind, which marks the difference between man and beast, is its capacity for contemplation and understanding. Any ape can deal with his immediate and momentary environment by instinctive reaction —as when he brushes a fly from his eyes—or even by figuring things out. That capacity to live in the universe, as I have called it for want of a better description, is man's alone. Having the power, however, a man must exercise it, or he will lose it and become a sick man because he is not a whole man. To remain physically well I have to use my arms and legs simply because I have the power to use them, even though automobiles and elevators remove the practical necessity. I must likewise exercise this other power, even though I live within the hive, if I am to remain a whole man. The difficulty is to reconcile the somnambulistic life of activity with that of contemplation and understanding. The daily activity and its context take possession of the mind to the exclusion of anything else. Here in the evening in my cell at home my mind continues to operate as it has all day in my office-cell, revolving the problems of the moment, which press in upon it and shut out everything else. If I should attempt to read a poem, however great, though it opened up all the dimensions and perspectives of the universe, it would mean nothing and leave me incredulous that it had been written at all and well regarded. It would not fit into my world. I cannot brush away the present, which obscures the universe as two pennies held over the eyes will hide the sky. I am oppressed and blinded by the imminence of these daily concerns. The doctor, who suffers from the same malady and has fallen into the somnambulism that it produces, cannot relieve me of this oppression. He gives me tonics to no purpose. I must get out of my cell, out of doors, out into the open world where I can see again.

Sometimes I have not known myself what I needed, or even that I needed anything. Of the ache in my soul I was hardly conscious, even as the wounded fish, being a dull creature, suffers from the barb in its side and does not know it. I tried to fill up the emptiness of my life with all the amusements that the hive offered, and turned on the radio in the evening to drive out the silence with noise. I could not let myself think with my conscious mind for fear of admitting that there was no purpose at all in spending my life. That the mass of men today suffer from this same emptiness and this seclusion from the light—leading lives of quiet desperation, as Thoreau puts it— is evidenced by the fact that our civilization goes to such lengths to provide public amusements and noise for its inmates. Instinctively we cherish the somnambulism to which the occupations and amusements of the hive contribute because it keeps us, like the fish, unconscious of our pain. The masters of imperial Rome knew the value of circuses as the Japanese conquerors in China knew the value of opium and encouraged its production. I have no doubt that the workers of another generation will have television in their cells.

To find oneself suddenly in the open after a long spell of confinement—like coming out of doors on a quiet starlit night from a noisy, crowded, smoke-filled room—is to experience revelation. Getting out into the open world, rediscovering the solitude and examining the distance, relieves the mind from the tight pressure of the present, cleans it, refreshes it, relaxes it and smooths it out, and so allows it to expand and admit through its subconscious part the universal understanding for which it was shaped. It is like awakening, after a nightmare, to find that all the darkness and horror was but a dream. This is reality, this meadowlark singing in the sunlight, not the artificial banging and clatter that, mistaken for life itself, had made life seem meaningless. To remind me of this, let me go down the river once a day and see the sunrise.

In this connection I have made another discovery. Although for years I have had to use my eyes intensively at short range from morning to night, they have continued to do me good service and I have not fallen into the necessity of encumbering my face with glasses. However, during the fall and winter of 1944-45, when my way of life kept me more closely confined than ever, it became increasingly apparent that they were giving out on me. The letters on a printed page, especially when I looked at them with my right eye only, appeared increasingly blurred, and sometimes I was no longer sure of recognizing my friends across the street. This caused me concern, for I did not wish to go through life with the most valuable of my five senses impaired or to be dependent on the optometrist and his prescriptions. Day after day I tested my eyes on the printed page or on signs posted about the city and marked their continuing deterioration. I was going to postpone as long as possible the evil day when I put on glasses that would confirm the impairment rather than cure it, but on evenings when I had to give up reading entirely it became plain that it was almost at hand.

It was in the second half of January, as I have said, that I began adventuring abroad, on Sundays, to see how the great ouside world was coming along, and it was then I made my discovery. After every excursion I found my eyes immediately repaired and for several days the letters of the printed page were sharp to my vision, which tended to grow murky again only toward the end of the week. When I began to go out every morning, as well as Sundays, my vision returned to its full clarity and so remained. Glasses could not have improved it.

There is no doubt about this discovery. For one thing, I could test the deterioration in my vision by the difference between my right eye and my left, which vanished after a few hours in the open peering at birds. I have since found that it returns and my vision begins to be blurred when I have not gone abroad for a number of weeks, and that it is always restored as completely by the same means. The conclusion is logical. Man's eyesight was adapted for use in the open, as a means of overcoming distance, but not for uninterrupted use indoors at close range. I hold this simple discovery, which others may have made as well, to be worth the entire industry by which optometrists and opticians live. It provides an additional reason for looking out upon the universe.

Oh ye! who have your eye-balls vexed and tired,
    Feast them upon the wideness of the sea . . .

———

The sun crossed the equator March 21, inaugurating the astronomical season of spring throughout the Northern Hemisphere. The days were now longer than the nights and, at the North Pole, the sun rose to remain for six months. In Washington the day was marked by cloudiness and that intermittent slanting rain which is a unique feature of spring. The wind is warm. The raindrops fall wide apart, if steadily, so that you walk out among them without really getting wet. Such a rain has a fresh, warm fragrance of its own, not to be described, that is the quintessence of spring. You could identify the season by your nose alone. A great blue heron was traveling high over the city, beating its big wings easily, on its way down-river to what destination or rendezvous I could not tell.

The rain was heavy next morning, whipped by a west wind. Bicycling along the embankment, I was buffeted by the gusts and flurries of rain. Three or four black ducks were riding the waves in the river, female mergansers were scattered in river and channel, a thousand gulls were feeding on the greensward at Hains Point. Through the rain, from the wind-swept expanses of turf, one heard the meadowlarks singing at intervals, that lonely song with its swooning melody, so very pure, simply a pair of syllables echoed once on a different pitch. The birds would sing out here and there, so that I was never beyond earshot of one or two. Startling in its suddenness: the excited

ki-ki-ki-ki-ki . . . of a killdeer taking off from the lawn, then the insistently repeated *killdée, killdée, killdée* . . . , diminishing in the distance and returning.

The next morning was cloudless and still. Over the river, near the foot of Anolastan Island, a compact flock of small gulls with white flashes in their wings were disporting in the dawnlight among the much larger ring-billed and herring gulls. The presence of these Bonaparte's gulls lightened the day for me, giving it the character of a special occasion.

————————

Sunday, March 25, because it brought the first warbler, long before I had expected it, stands out in the list of days. In the sunrise a milky mist was steaming up from the river, like a smoke screen laid along the channel. The dew was still sparkling on the grass and visible as a soft radiance or ground mist over it. Today the singing of birds was everywhere continuous and uninterrupted; where before today the orchestra had

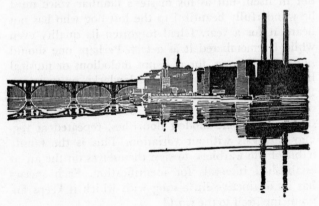

simply been tuning up, the individual instruments sounding separately. From either side of the road, as I bicycled through the misty dawnlight, came the song of the field sparrow, beginning slowly, all on one pitch, a series of measured notes accelerating until the bird was trilling like a canary. Thoreau knew this song a hundred years ago, and from his description it is apparent that there has been no change, though so many sparrow generations have elapsed that it would take man from two to three thousand years to equal them. It is as though Homer still sang.

I had already put up my bicycle, preparatory to going out into the marsh at Dyke, in fact I had climbed the roadside fence and was on my way, when I heard a song from the trees across the highway that transfixed me. I knew it well, and my subconscious being was immediately flooded with the recognition and the old associations that accompanied it, though my consciousness fumbled and for the moment I could not say what it was. I stood rooted to the spot with delight and wonder. To me the song was beautiful, not in itself, but as his master's familiar voice must be wonderfully beautiful to the lost dog who has not heard it for a year. I had forgotten its quality even while I remembered it as a fact. Perhaps one should not call it a song, for it is not melodious or musical like the songs of thrushes, meadowlarks, or sparrows. It is simply an insectlike notation in sound, a brief signature made up of two or three preliminary strokes and some modest flourishes, repeated at regular intervals without variation. This is the family habit of the warblers, to sign themselves on the air at established intervals for identification. Each species has its distinctive little song with which it keeps announcing itself to the world.

I found my bird quickly enough, through my binoculars, in the bare tops of the trees, flitting from twig to branch, from branch to trunk, from trunk to branch again, intent on its business, peering under and over and about, pausing only at the established intervals to throw back its head and make its announcement with vibrating bill. The low morning sun shone full upon it among the treetops, the bright yellow throat, like a piece of the sun itself, the blue-gray wings, the black-and-white head of the yellow-throated warbler. Now that it was here, the warbler season had begun.

The family of wood warblers inhabits the New World exclusively, having no close relatives or parallels abroad. However, when the first settlers came to this country from England they brought with them the names of English birds to fasten, without any fine discrimination, onto the American birds. They called our big red-breasted thrush the robin, after the English redbreast or robin redbreast, and they called these dazzling little birds, the like of which they had never seen, warblers, though they do not warble at all and, for the most part, have songs like the buzzing and creaking of insects. These little birds are the principal glory of the North American spring, quick and dainty in their movements, incessantly active, as bright and varied in color as the butterflies. For a few weeks in spring, on their way north, they swarm through our woods, filling and transforming them with their variety and numbers. Each of the many species is distinct in its color and markings, each has its own vocal signature, which the observer comes to recognize in time, each is a separate object of delight. Coming from the tropics, they arrive with the first appearance of leaves on the trees, reach the peak of their abundance about the time the trees achieve their full foliage, and then diminish rapidly until only those that nest here remain. The flowering of the Japanese cherry trees is not so wonderful as the wave of warblers that passes through the countryside in mid-May, remaining sometimes only a day.

Earlier naturalists could not know the warblers as we know them, since they did not have the prism binoculars that are necessary to observe these quick little birds among the leaves in the treetops. For the most part they must have been aware only of innumerable little birds darting in and out among the trees and the abundance and variety of song that accompanied them. They knew the beauty of the individual birds chiefly by bringing them down with a gun and examining them in the hand, but here they missed all the beauty of their ways, the extreme delicacy and quickness of their flitting and fluttering movements.

The appreciation of warblers is a slow acquisition, since most of the species are to be seen and heard only for a few days each year, and the rarer may be seen only at intervals of several years. When I say that I have been acquainted with a warbler for ten years, it may be that the sum of that acquaintance is only a few minutes. Perhaps I have seen the bird and heard its song only a half-dozen times, and then when I was distracted by the presence of its innumerable congeners. The appreciation of birds, indeed the appreciation of all the phenomena of spring, cannot be dissociated from the accumulations of memory. The appearance of a familiar bird immediately awakens a train of forgotten associations, and this makes each spring transcend its predecessor. The interest accumulates and is compounded. The first yellow-throated warbler next year will be the more meaningful to me as it brings back that moment in the woods opposite Dyke. For one remembers clearly enough the fact of such a moment, but only an evocative sight or sound or smell can bring back the full emotion. The person who sees the bird for the first time cannot know what moves me.

The bird, or the event, must have a background to be appreciated, but not necessarily the background of one's individual memory alone, important as this is. It is the great function of nature, literature and art to

teach us how to see these things, for the beauty of an object, a song, or a dance can never be altogether intrinsic, independent of old associations and acquired understanding. I have never seen an upland plover, or heard its cry, but the experience when it comes will be the more meaningful for me because I shall recall that description of the bird as Hudson knew it, flying over the pampas on its long migration to North America. "Lying awake in bed," he wrote, "I would listen by the hour to that sound coming to me from the sky, mellowed and made beautiful by distance and the profound silence of the moonlit world, until it acquired a fascination for me above all sounds on earth, so that it lived ever after in me. . . . It was the sense of mystery it conveyed which so attracted and impressed me —the mystery of that delicate, frail, beautiful being, traveling in the sky, alone, day and night, crying aloud at intervals as if moved by some powerful emotion, beating the air with its wings, its beak pointing like the needle of the compass to the north, flying, speeding on its seven-thousand-mile flight to its nesting home in another hemisphere." Thus I am furnished by Hudson with a vicarious memory of the bird, in lieu of personal experience.

This fact, that one must have a background in memory for the appreciation of birds, was first brought home to me when I first visited the American tropics and looked on birds as wonderful in their characters, their colors and movements, as any to be seen in the world. But there was nevertheless a strange emptiness and frustration in the experience. These were not my birds, I could not really know them at all, or know how to see them, at first sight. It was only with the lapse of time and the building up of my own recollected associations that I began to appreciate and understand them. I could not be moved by a cotinga as I was when, riding through uninhabited tropical forest, surrounded by parrots and toucans, with monkeys in the trees overhead, I came upon the familiar sight of a wintering catbird and watched it flitting among the tropical vines or catching caterpillars on the jungle floor. There is no delight like that of recognition.

The case would have been different had I gone to England instead, for the bird life of England, while it may be intrinsically the poorest to be found in any like region of the world, has the richest background of any in its literary associations, which is to say in the accumulated recollections of sensitive men over many generations. These accumulated associations and memories of an entire people form a background for the song of the nightingale. When I go into the woods with someone who does not share them, and listen to the song of a bird, I am sometimes struck by the fact that he hears something altogether different from what I hear. His ear is differently attuned. One must share common memories in order to share common experiences.

———

Having just said that our predecessors could not know the warblers as we do, knowing them only in the hand, I have had an experience to show me that I, for my part, have never before known the warblers as they did. Now—the date being October 21, 1945—I hold in the hollow of my hand the body of a little bird killed last night in its migration by flying against a railing atop the roof. I saw it lying in the sunlight on

the tarred roof this morning, when I went up there, a creature hardly larger than a mouse, with flaming gold breast streaked with black, and gold elsewhere or russet blending into brown and black. It has a slender, pointed black bill. Its fragile, polished black feet simply hang from it, the toes grasping nothing. You would be surprised, holding it in your hand, at

how soft and thick is its coat of feathers. The plumage
is most of the bird, for the body is simply a small hard
core at the center which you feel with your fingers
pinching through the downy mass. Surely this is some
creature of art, created in a hothouse by a magician
and raised on nectar fed it at the end of a hair! But
human artistry has produced nothing to compare to
this. The domestic canary is grossness incarnate by
comparison. The magic that produced this complete
creature, this little world in itself, really does surpass
all understanding.

I recall a Chinese painting on silk that shows a man
starting back in surprise and utter delight as, having
taken the lid from a box in his hand, a white crane
with outstretched neck and trailing legs escapes in
flight. One looks at this delicate creature with the same
surprise and wonder. It would serve the purpose of
worship better than the bones of any martyr. Yet, fine
as it is, in life it knew wind, rain, and storm from the
islands of the Caribbean to the forests of Canada, and
traveled farther about the world, under its own power,
than most men. A man could not survive such exposure, or match it in feats of hardihood. This warbler, during this past spring that I have been describ-
ing, traveled northward from the Caribbean on his
own, singing his thin *zee-zee-zee-zee* by day from the
treetops, flying over the world by night, to nest in
some wind-raked spruce by the swampy edge of a forest in Ontario or New Brunswick or Maine. He molted
before his return migration this fall, and even the gos-
samer downy tips of those radiant feathers are not
worn off yet, despite the thousand or more miles he
must have flown to reach here. When I see men able
to pass by such a shining and miraculous thing as this
Cape May warbler, the very distillate of life, and then
marvel at the internal-combustion engine, I think we
had all better make ourselves ready for another Flood.

I am convinced that this world of man's greatness is antediluvian.

King Louis the Pious was at Doué in Aquitaine when, in 814, he received the news that the Emperor Charlemagne, his father, had died. "Making such speed as he could," writes Professor Oman, "he arrived at Aachen after a journey of thirty days, and took possession of the reins of power." The village of Doué, as the crow flies, is some three hundred and eighty miles from Aachen; yet Louis, making such speed as he could, took thirty days to cover the distance. I have hunted in vain through volumes of scholarship for some description of what the land that is now France actually looked like during the Dark Ages. It was already ancient in terms of human habitation; having supported Cro-Magnon Man in the late stages of the Glacial Period; having been inhabited, a thousand years before Charlemagne's death, by those Gauls who worshiped under oak trees at the sign of the mistletoe; having known the military and administrative officials of Rome, the transient hordes of Vandals and Goths, and the Frankish ancestors of Charlemagne who had come down from the north, under Childerich and Chlodovech, to make it their kingdom. It had been farmed for the Lord knows how many centuries. Yet it must have been wilderness in 814, and such Roman roads as had been built across it had long since become ruins for archaeologists, had there been any. I suppose King Louis and his followers, impatient to seize the reins of imperial power, rode through gloomy forests, alert for wild boars and bears, for the great antlered elk and the wolf packs, awakened in their encampments at night by the screams of eagle owls or the soft *tu-who, tu-whit tu-who* of the little tawny owl. Like as not, as they approached the Loire they had to skirt endless marshes in which they disturbed the waterfowl, and were days riding up the bank of the river, through the miasmal mists of the valley, to find a crossing. Or perhaps they built rafts that could carry the horses and baggage. It was not as the crow flies for Louis—or as the airplane that makes it from Doué to Aachen in an hour. There was jubilation when, after days of alternate drizzle and downpour—not a man but was wet to the bone, including the king, all of them grumbling maledictions on the weather—the sun broke through and at the same time they emerged on open uplands where horses and men had firm footing. At each settlement along the way (they could locate them several miles ahead by the kites that towered in the sky over them) the chief tribesman, with his escort, came out to do obeisance and to receive rough instructions from minor officials as to precisely what the royal party would require by way of entertainment. There was requisitioning, and perhaps trouble with the women.

When King Louis and his band at last rode through the gates at Aachen, after thirty days' march, they did so with a great display of pomp, carefully prepared in advance, for it was necessary to impress the court and intimidate those who felt inward revulsions at the thought of the pious Louis picking up the spear of the old man whom they had venerated from infancy. But the historian has not recorded what a pitifully small spectacle this was in the wilderness. Hardly less than the waterfowl, these men inhabited an unhuman world. The frontier was three feet off the road on either side.

Five hundred years earlier, the misty land of Britain, away off in the northern ocean, had been more civilized than it was at the time Charlemagne died. The rule of Rome, its power weakening with time and with distance, had overcome the south of Britain but had exhausted itself on the borders of the Caledonian wilderness. Here a spectacular frontier was visibly established, known to history as Hadrian's Wall, built of stone and extending across the breadth of the island from the Irish to the North Sea. "Just when you think you are at the world's end, you see a smoke from East to West as far as the eye can turn, and then, under it, also as far as the eye can stretch, houses and temples, shops and theaters, barracks and granaries, trickling like dice behind—always behind—one long, low, rising and falling, and hiding and showing line of towers. And that is the Wall!" This is how Kipling described it, through the mouth of a Roman centurion. "Thirty feet high is the Wall, and on the Picts' side, the North, is a ditch, strewn with blades of old swords and spear-heads set in wood, and tyres of wheels joined by chains. . . . On one side heather, woods and ruins where Picts hide, and on the other, a vast town . . ." This was a frontier that, while it was manned, even a rabbit could not slip across. The centurion of the Thirtieth soon learned on the Wall to "take Heather," this being his way of escaping from the noisy and sordid life of the town. "Taking Heather" means "Going out hunting in the Pict

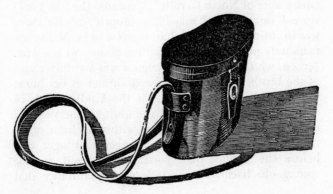

country with a tame Pict. You are quite safe so long as you are his guest, and wear a sprig of heather where it can be seen."

This custom of taking the heather I can understand, since it is my custom too. Granted, the scene has changed in its details. Instead of the heather in my cap, a pair of binoculars is my badge. The town is Washington in 1945, with its gaming and bureaucracy. The wilderness is at hand, its frontier the edge of every marsh, meadow, and woodland lot. I know how Parnesius the centurion felt, escaping from the uproar and stench to follow the trail of the dog wolf across the bogs, or of the "great red deer with horns like Jewish candlesticks."

There is, as you might expect, a freemasonry among those of us who take the heather. We already know each other by the badge when we meet, and enter into conversation without introduction, talking like old friends of our common preoccupation. More than that, we trust one another like brothers and constitute a mutual-aid society. Take the example, which I cherish gratefully in memory, of the lonely soldier who arrived for a weekend leave at Chapel Hill, N.C., after an unremitting month of drill on the barren fields of Fort Bragg. Having no acquaintance in the entire state of North Carolina, I entered the first bookstore I came to and asked the proprietor who there was in town who professed an interest in birds. He immediately put me in touch, by telephone, with a Mrs. Jensen, who, as soon as she knew I was a stranger and of the brotherhood, invited me to dinner at her home in the outlying countryside. At the kindly hands of the Jensen family I enjoyed the most unreserved and spontaneous hospitality, so that within an hour of arriving at Chapel Hill I was no longer a stranger and, before the evening had passed, felt myself at ease among old friends, in a circle of acquaintance that

widened with repeated visits. That badge bespeaks
mutual trust, as between Pict and Pict, Roman and
Roman, or Pict and Roman. It is one brotherhood the
country over, and I daresay the world over.

———————

This digression—which, looked at in the large, is no
digression at all, though it has led me through Gaul,
Britain, and North Carolina—still leaves me in the
sunrise at the edge of the woods, watching the gold-
throated warbler hunting and flitting about the treetops, periodically uttering its established signal. From
the trees on the other side of the roadway, a repeated,
high-pitched, nasal *vee* announced the arrival of the
first blue-gray gnatcatcher. I was not alone to greet
these newcomers, but with a little band, all wearing
the insignia: two men, a woman, and a little girl. The
Touseys were Bostonians, and it was quite natural
for me to receive from them, though I had never seen
them before, the latest news of my friends in Boston.
At their invitation I abandoned my bicycle and such
plans as I had for the day to join in a visit by automobile to Lebanon, an area of wooded and marshy
wilderness at the head of a deep inlet below Mount
Vernon, which Dr. Paul Bartsch of the Smithsonian
Institution has posted as a sanctuary for wildlife.

———————

Sing to me, Muse, of the Marshes of Lebanon, on
Gunston Cove below Pohick, under the sun-gilded uplands of Accotink! Here in this vale is the home of the
eagle. Leaving the Richmond highway by the left
hand, the road runs through old farmland with
orchards and wood lots. Dr. Bartsch, at the age of sev-
enty-five, is with his own hands restoring an old brick

house that stands in open fields at the brink of a wooded slope. Here he welcomes all of the brotherhood, who need no invitation. In the twilight of his years, after a lifetime of accumulating honors by labor, he has moved to the frontier and embarked on a new enterprise in the wilderness. Lebanon is a sanctuary for wildfowl, and incidentally for those who take the heather. Dr. Bartsch is Allo the Pict. In ancient work clothes, accompanied by one or two helpmeets and by two miniature parrots of a strange species, he hands you the Visitors' or Domesday Book to sign. The wilderness is then yours.

It is March 25 and the dawn of summer. A light bloom of green, as insubstantial as a mist, is on the distant, wooded hillsides now. The dogwood is on the verge of blossoming. In the moist darkness of the woods, some violets in a clump are just about to open. You hesitate to turn away from them. An old wagon track leads down and down through woods of Virginia pine, joining with other tracks and occasionally forking, to your confusion if you are not careful. A musical chippering, all on one pitch, of established duration and regular interval, comes from this side and then that. This is the song of the newly arrived pine warbler, the streaked brown and yellow mite, throwing his head back amid the bowers of pine needles and singing with vibrating bill.

At the bottom of the slope lies a long open marsh sunk into the woods, with trees wading out from the borders ankle-deep in bog water. Here, overlooking the marsh, is a slight elevation with ancient gnarled beeches, and tumbled rocks to sit on, a Wagnerian stage setting. The sounds of the forge and the cry of *Nothung, Nothung!* would not be out of place. Instead, a hairy woodpecker utters a machine-gun burst of notes; two wood ducks, barely seen behind the trees, rocket away, crying *oo-eek, oo-eek* . . . A heron

has taken off silently and wings its way along the edge
of the forest. This, obviously, is the spot for our pic-
nic lunch, or for a sacrifice to the gods. You feel like a
hero in it. What could be more appropriate, then,
than that our binoculars should fix an eagle soaring
over the trees at the far end of the marsh?—not the
American eagle, bird of the New World, but the
golden eagle of emperors, heraldic symbol of feudal
Europe. That glint on its head is the gold of the Nie-

belung hoard, the gold of fallen empires. Tamerlane
knew it on the steppes of Asia. Forty centuries look
down upon you from that brow. Now the imperial
bird soars upward and away, farther and farther, till
it is lost to sight.

At its lower end, by way of a narrow neck through
the infringing woods, this marsh opens into the main
marsh, the long, sweeping, sunlit vista of reeds and
rivulets, between the high hills, that in turn gives onto
Gunston Cove. While the company keeps inside the
woods where the footing is firm, I choose to wade
knee-deep on the outside through cold water and
quagmire, where I can see about me. The greater yel-

lowlegs, one here and one there, are calling in their excitement from open mud flats. This, however, is pre-eminent as the home of the American eagles. They break from the big trees at the border as we advance, flapping with slow beat across the open, soaring into the sky. I count eleven in sight at one time, and there are more. One folds its wings and falls from the sky upon another, which almost at the moment of collision rolls over in one complete revolution, letting the attacker glance by; then both flap upward to see which, this time, shall rise above the other. These are giants at play. Another, white head and white tail gleaming in the sunlight, drops to the sparkling surface of the cove, splashes, and makes off with a fish in its talons.

Somewhere in the mists of time the eagle and the warbler had a common ancestor. Now the warbler sings in the pine woods, the eagle soars above the marshes, the ducks swim in the bay, gulls wheel. How extraordinary if this were altogether uninspired! We live ourselves in the mists of time, and cannot cast our vision beyond it. The world of our senses is purely spectacular.

———————

Every season is exceptional, and this spring was no exception. Flower and foliage were well ahead of schedule, and the warblers with them. During the week of March 25 to April 1 the woods everywhere were springing into leaf. You could see in the morning how much the leaves had grown overnight. This, of course, was measurable, and I measured it. In two days the leaves of a tulip tree had more than doubled their size and were already some two inches across. Like everything else, they responded to and were the outward manifestations of the perennial life that was flowing and surging in the earth. We take this for granted because so we have always seen it happen, just as the starlings heading for the city in the late afternoon take it for granted that night will fall. We make provision like the starlings, and buy our summer clothes in late winter. The starlings, of course, take these things for granted because they have not the gift of questioning and contemplation. Modern men often take life and the seasons for granted because they fondly believe that science has the explanations, that everything is known. In the same way we used to believe, when little, that grownups knew the answers to all questions. Hence no mystery! Science, however, follows back along the chain of physical causation to the brink of darkness and discovers nothing. It simply takes more steps to reach the unknown. The scientist who has explored the farthest is the most likely to believe in gods and demons. For most of us, however, living our somnambulistic lives, anything will do by way of explanation. Spring is the season when the leaves come out, said the old man, and the leaves come out because it is spring. For this and like observations he was accounted a philosopher in his circle.

I knew a lady who was willing to leave it to the Supreme Court of the United States whether there was a God.

On March 27, the day that the first swallow appeared on the Tidal Basin, a roughwing, two violets bloomed in a crack in the paving of Rock Creek Parkway. I thought then that I could view the crumbling of our civilization with equanimity if violets were to spring up in the cracks. They would, too. All the flower shops in Washington do not hold as many flowers as may someday grow naturally here, out of the stonework. The mark of mortality is on everything man builds, but the violets and their kind are immortal. The vast and busy cities that once flourished in

Central America are hardly to be found under the masses of foliage and bloom that cover them today, though the men who occupied them appeared to have conquered the wilderness. The government officials speeding to work past this spot in the early morning, if they only knew, would regard this clump of violets with awe. It was not planted by the United States Park Service.

Heat, summer clouds, and sunshine, with sudden brief showers, marked the days of this week. On March 30 a robin was testing a newly made nest in a magnolia bush near the Jefferson Memorial. On March 31 a loon flew past the Capitol dome on its way north. Large, milling, screaming flocks of ring-billed gulls passed over the State Department, going north. The number of gulls about the city had diminished since the first week in March, and now those remaining were mostly immature birds. Flickers in Potomac Park were displaying grotesquely and "whickering" before one another. More swallows came into the city. The slow, immemorial change and revolution of the seasons was continuing in spite of human alarms and excursions on the face of the earth. The essential stability of nature stood in contrast to the impermanence of man's architecture.

———————

(On Sunday, March 26, 1786, George Washington made the following entry in his diary at Mount Vernon: "The warmth of yesterday and this day, forwarded vegetation much; the buds of some trees, particularly the Weeping Willow and Maple, had displayed their leaves and blossoms and all others were swelled and many ready to put forth.")

Easter Sunday, April 1, was a golden day. The stars and a waning moon were out when I left for my excursion by bicycle down the river. In the darkness by the Shoreham Hotel the robins were already caroling in chorus, anticipating the daybreak. The sun rose in classic splendor as I passed the airport—as it had risen among the Aegean isles three thousand years ago (the golden-throned dawn) for a lonely wanderer striving to return to his home, as it had risen a thousand years ago over the misty valley of the Loire. Robins, titmice, wrens, sparrows, thrashers, cardinals, goldfinches, purple finches were all singing. At Dyke, in the sparkling haze and freshness of the new day, a pair of wood ducks flew clamoring from the big trees beside the road, circled, landed in the trees again, took off again. Other wood ducks, in pairs, flew through the trees or out over the marshes. Pine warblers, yellow-throated warblers, blue-gray gnatcatchers, and newly arrived black-and-white warblers contributed their notes to the dawn.

A week ago I had marked the first green bloom on the woods. Now, to my eager imagination, it seemed virtually summer, the trees in flower and foliage, though one could still see through them. Later in the season the leaves would hang in heavy masses, obscuring the view. Today they were still young and tender on the trees. The borders of the woods were everywhere illuminated by the white dogwood, the pink dogwood, and the brilliant redbud, now in full flower. Near Mount Vernon I came upon Roger Peterson and a friend, out with cameras and tripods to make color photographs of the redbud. Peterson told me the flower and foliage was between two and three weeks ahead of last year's dates, basing his calculation on the blooming of the magnolias, now over. Who could remember such an early spring as this, with everything so far ahead of schedule? At Fort Belvoir young horned larks had left their nest two weeks ago.

(On April 21, 1785, Washington at Mount Vernon wrote in his diary: "The Sassafras not yet full out, nor the Redbud—Dogwood blossom still inclosed in the button." Two days later he wrote: "The Dogwood buttons were just beginning to open as the Redwood (or bud) blossom, for though they had appeared several days the blossoms had not expanded.")

On the morning of April 3, after a night of storm, the Bonaparte's gulls were moving north along the surface of the river as far as the eye could reach, flicking their wings, sparkling in the early sunlight. They acquire their summer plumage as the trees their foliage, and through my glasses I could see that some now had black heads while the heads of others were still white or mottled. Men, it occurred to me, are among the few creatures that undergo no seasonal changes. We don't even grow shaggy coats in winter.

That morning a Louisiana water-thrush sang loud, clear and repeatedly from a ravine in Rock Creek Park as I bicycled to work. *Tzee, tzee, tzee, tzippy-tzippy-tzip* he sang, with emphasis, so that I should think one could have heard him half a mile off. (Birds that haunt rushing streams have loud voices to rise above the uproar.) Brown thrashers were singing in the city now—really singing, for they are among the birds that do not merely emit signals but are musicians, con-

sciously practicing their art, as if inspired to transcend their own mortality and achieve a heaven that lies, surely, just beyond mortal reach. One that sang constantly on Woodland Drive had a whole orchestra of bells and woodwinds in his throat. His song, every phrase with its echo, bubbled like a natural spring breaking from the ground in flood season. Yet there was a method in it, a repetition and return to the same themes. Before the week was out, barn swallows, spotted sandpipers, and ruddy ducks in Washington Channel had been added to the list of new birds.

This week, however, was bountiful chiefly in its flowers. The City of Washington might have been deliberately decked for a flower festival, as when the citizens hang out their flags because it is Flag Day. The lilac clusters came out in profusion overnight, among the young leaves, freshening the air. So did the azaleas, in all their variety, transforming the woodland parks and dooryards. A man from Mars might have stopped passers-by to inquire in what god's celebration the city was so garlanded.

This is the height of spring—or one of the heights, to be followed by others. Yet it would be improvident to find only spring in springtime or fall in autumn. There is no better time than winter to enjoy a summer day, no better time than spring to savor the fall. If you observe the progress of the seasons carefully, you will find them all present the year around. They are interwoven themes in this continuing symphonic utterance, each becoming dominant in its turn without ever wholly vanquishing the rest. Listen carefully and you will hear on the cellos, throughout this first movement, the theme of fall; subordinate, awaiting its eventual turn to be announced on the brasses and taken up by the violins, but there nevertheless. Occasionally and for a moment it emerges clearly, as if by accident, like a bird that sings out of season.

The day after the lilacs and azaleas came out full, I was awakened long before dawn by the wind lashing the trees outside and the rattling of my bedroom door. A gale from the northwest, blowing in gusts, tossed the river and Tidal Basin. Black clouds traveled overhead, intermittent showers drenched the earth. In East Potomac Park the ground was littered with twigs from the bobbing and tugging willows. About the Tidal Basin and on 17th Street the leaves were not falling but the elm seeds were, whirling down on the wind and drifting along the street. They drove into your face, as you pedaled against the wind, pelting it in showers. Who ever heard of being blinded by elm seeds? By afternoon the sky had cleared except for traveling powder puffs, the wind had steadied and came from the west, and it grew cold. A perfect fall day. The elm seeds, like some breakfast cereal, lay along the gutters in drifts. During the next few days the street cleaners were busy sweeping them up and carting them away—lest, perhaps, they sprout in the macadam and the streets become forested. The street cleaners were dutifully defending our civilization, guarding it from ruin, though they overlooked the threat of violets that I had happened to discover.

It is a fascination to me to find the wilderness everywhere interpenetrating our civilization. Even the prisoner enclosed by stone and macadam may breathe the freedom of the frontier if he can but look out at a piece of the sky above. The other day toward sunset (it being now the fall season), my eye caught against the sky over the city what appeared to be the faintest

wisp of smoke, so faint and wispy I could hardly be
sure it was not a wisp of imagination. But through
powerful binoculars that wisp became a dense flock
of wildfowl moving, almost imperceptibly south. I

took my binoculars from my eyes and then, search as
I might, could no longer find it. Instead my eye caught
a thread, distinctly seen if one concentrated, against
another part of the blue overhead. The glasses showed
clearly eight Canada geese strung out in single file,
moving south, one behind the other, beating their
great wings easily, shifting their formation so that

now they were in line oblique, now again in file, creeping across the sky. These geese, at such an altitude over the city that they were all but invisible to the naked eye (how many remain quite invisible?), were on their way, perhaps, from the tundras of the arctic to wintering grounds on the coasts of Virginia and North Carolina. It may be that they had taken wing that morning from some lake tributary to Hudson Bay, and would later splash down in the silver moonlight on the waters of the Rappahannock. So marvelous is the flight of geese to men who love freedom! Unseen by earthlings, these eight travel over cities and farms and factories, alone in space. Above city streets thronged with traffic, above roadhouses where dancing couples shake their feet to the music of jukeboxes, above the club car at the end of the train in which the Director studies the Director's Report, above the factory hand releasing steam from the boiler, above the arguments of the orator, above the talk of the hour, above the fashions of the moment—above all this they travel serenely, secure and free in the endless blue, seeming hardly to move, so high they are, beating their wings, bearing ever south. . . . They are dependent on no one's hospitality, on no machine—almost, it seems, not on the earth itself. It is likely that in all their journey only one of the ant swarm below chances to see them; and that, passing high above Washington as they have already passed high over Ottawa and over Harrisburg, they for their part see only the confluence of two glimmering rivers.

I should like to have called the attention of the senators on Capitol Hill to these geese overhead, as to the violets that had grown up without a by-your-leave in the parkway. (Geese have before this been a portent to senators.) Here, in a way, the geese above and the lawmakers below, are earthly travelers that pass each other as if they belonged to other dimen-

sions. There is no exchange of signals, no correspondence, no recognition between them—the aboriginal
and eternal wilderness on the one hand, on the other
the passing carnival of civilization. How many city
dwellers, in their somnambulistic preoccupation, ever
know that wild geese are overhead, or violets under-
foot in the crack of the pavement? The city is threatened with invasion from every side.

It is a fair estimate that it would have taken the
geese six or seven hours from Doué to Aachen, in
contrast to the thirty days that Louis the Pious
needed. Today we can better the time of the geese,
but at the cost of our individual independence. Like
Faust in his compact with Mephistopheles, we have
sold our souls for the power to do it.

> Yea, stranger engines for the brunt of war,
> Than was the fiery keel at Antwerp's bridge,
> I'll make my servile spirits to invent.

Faust, you recall, was distracted from the effort to
achieve his natural perfection by the seductive
thought of power. He wanted to free himself from
nature, to subject natural forces to his command, to
fly in a dragon-drawn chariot through the empyrean.
Because he cared more about this than about preserv-
ing and perfecting his soul, Mephistopheles was able
to bargain for that soul. In the legend as it has been
transmitted through the generations, Faust, when his
time was up, was seized and dragged down into the
conflagration of chaos. Only Goethe, in his own ren-
dition, envisaged the ultimate salvation of Faust
through the regeneration of his moral sense and the
consequent abandonment of his obsession.

Now, this is pure legend, and so it is more real and
more true than anything you will find in the history
books. For history is the record of facts that may or
may not reveal truth, but legend is the portrayal of

truth itself as men have known it. The legend of the damnation of Faust has persisted in varying guises from earliest times (one version takes place in the Garden of Eden) because it communicates the experience. . . .

But these are autumn thoughts, not to be labored here.

————————

I never heard of anyone who set himself up as a connoisseur of sunrises, though there are many to display a cultivated appreciation of such sunrises as hang on gallery walls. I do not quarrel with them, but for my

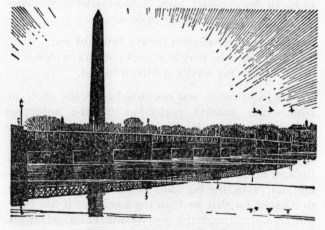

own part I have chosen the original. I am a connoisseur of sunrises and sunsets, ground mists, cloud patterns, big and little rains, moonlight, gusts and gales, skies, and all varieties of weather and landscapes. If need be, I could cock my head and squint my eye as shrewdly as any Master of Arts. I could tell you what is lacking or overdone. Let anyone try to compete with me, I could sigh and exclaim in one breath with the best of them. I could tell when a landscape "holds its place" or is "exquisitely realized."

I would know when to encourage nature with my praise and when to admonish. Only, nature differs from art in this, that all the demands are made on the critic. He must himself know how to hold his place.

"I accept the universe!" Margaret Fuller announced to her friends. "Gad, she'd better!" was Carlyle's comment. "Roll on, O world!" exclaimed the poet; whereupon the world rolled on.

The most delicate and lovely sunrises, I think, are those that shine through a ground mist, burning it off as the new day is established. The mist may be only a haziness between trees, or it may be a white cloud that lies full length upon the ground. It vanishes shortly after the sun discovers it.

Such a cloud rested upon the river the morning of April 8, spilling over its banks and billowing onto the parkway. In the half-light of dawn, skimming down the parkway on my bicycle, I passed in and out through its bossy contours, one moment seeing my way, the next bathed in cloud mist. So it must have been with Athene when from the heights of Olympus she came glancing down to stand in the land of Ithaca. The cloud mist became radiant and then dazzling as the sun rose. It was becoming transparent, burning away, as I approached Dyke; but still clinging among the trees, which stood like ghosts in its dimness. It was as though, by miraculous dispensation, one stood before the Creation itself, witness to the original emergence of earth from darkness and swirling mists. Multitudes of birds, like an angelic chorus, were singing in the landscape as it took form. This was Paradise regained, man standing in its midst like Adam in the first awakening.

This daily renewal of the Creation, like the annual renewal, is not appreciated among us. It is a fact that every dawn gives us a new chance, restores our innocence, if only we will realize it. However jaded the earth may become in the course of each day, it begins the next day with a fresh start. And so might all mankind. This renewal is an utterly wonderful thing. It is salvation itself.

Youth and the challenge of youth, the innocence and the glory, all fade. The earth begins with a miracle, but quickly settles down to business. By five minutes after the hour, such is man's preoccupation with the present, he ceases to believe even in the possibility of a miracle. He is a skeptic before midday, a cynic by afternoon, a nihilist by evening. But as I stand before this sunrise, and while it lingers in my memory, one question persists: If this is not an altogether beneficent world, how comes it to be so full of music and light? how account for this? It does no good at all to explain to me the facts of mist and the nature of light, and why the birds sing. I know why the birds sing, but I do not know why they sing beautifully. That is the crux of the matter. If the purpose of the thrasher's song is only to warn rival males that he is in his home territory and will defend it, then he might as well croak. Here in the dawn, I think I have been mistaken all this time in regarding the earth as a place of tears and tribulation for men aspiring to an imagined heaven. This earth itself is our heaven. As for the philosophers and scientists, they have explained nothing to me since they have not explained why the earth should be beautiful. They are old men of the evening; they long for heaven because they face the grave.

Item: Out of the luminous mist in which the trees showed like ghosts I heard the forgotten voice of yesteryear—once and silence, again and silence, and again—at regular intervals from a grove of trees, the little buzzing, ascending wisp of song that the parula warbler gives off. I found him to look at, flitting and peering among the dewy leaves in the treetops, freshly arrived from the Indies to attend the rites of spring in the land of his birth; here for the dawn of creation.

Last week the marshes of Dyke still showed only the gray stalks of last year's reeds. Today the new green reeds and a teeming variety of marsh plants were burgeoning everywhere, proliferating, crowding upward. I waded out among them from the edge of the woods, putting up masses of ducks into the sun so that I saw them only as flitting shades against the misty glare, and heard their gabbling voices. I thought better of that, retreated, and came around on the long spit along the eastern edge, outflanking them. Three greater yellowlegs were chasing wildly over the marshes in circles, here and gone again and back again, this way and that, filling the landscape with their excited cries. They put down on a mudbank—one, two, three—standing delicately upon their long legs, wings still extended, still opening their bills to cry . . . then off again with no warning, this way and that over the marshes. The mist had been evanescing under the sun and now was only a haze. The warmth of the sun could be felt.

Six pair of blue-winged teal, male and female, swam about at leisure in a broad inlet almost at my feet, dabbling with their bills in the still water. The two nearest leaped from the water, flew about twenty yards, and put down again, the ripples from their landings one after another crossing one another. Two baldpates, also dipping and dabbling with their bills, floated out from the grasses to join them. It was a sort of pageant.

Elsewhere the blue-winged teal were flying in little groups; not heavily like the black ducks, but sharply like the yellowlegs, skimming down to the surface, swinging wide about the bends of inlets, rising and falling, finally passing behind the trees or dropping out of sight. You would never think, to see them so peaceful on the water, that they had this wildness of flight in them. Yet here they are, borne on their own wings from the tropics, perhaps from far below the equator, freshly arrived, stopping over for a day or a week in the outskirts of Washington on their way, like as not, to Great Slave Lake in the Canadian Northwest or some river marsh in Alaska.

A blue-winged teal banded in Quebec in the fall of

1930 was killed less than four weeks later in British
Guiana, more than 2,500 miles distant—having perhaps put in at Dyke on the way, to float serenely atop
his reflection, to dip and dabble, to splash and bathe
in the morning sunlight, or to skim with his companions high and low over the fields of marsh grass. The
city fathers are remiss, it seems to me, in their neglect
of these occasions. Perhaps a special flag should be run
up over the Capitol dome to signal the arrival of such
distinguished visitors.

From the spit an elevated plank catwalk extends
across the marsh to the brink of an inlet, so that one
walks like an angel, dry-shod and untouched, through
the midst of the watery wilderness. This is the attribute of divinity, to be in the world but not of it.
There is no floundering here. The red-winged black-

birds are beside themselves with curiosity and excitement at this visitation. They cling to the swaying reeds
all about, clucking and whistling, take flight, hover,
circle, and put down again, seizing the reeds with their
feet and swinging on them. They whistle and cluck
in sheer astonishment, hardly knowing whether to be
alarmed. Men would behave the same, I think, if an
angel stepped out on a cloud above their city.

At the end of the catwalk I have the best view of
the teal and the baldpates, and a drake wood duck
now, floating in perfect serenity on the surface of a
mirror. From moment to moment the three yellowlegs, still crying, shoot past, cutting the air with their
pointed wings, sweeping wide over the marsh in circles and arabesques like cosmic ice skaters.

From the reeds, almost at my feet, a great streaked
brown bird bursts up and flaps away across the marsh,
grumbling and grunting for all the world like a fat
man out of breath. When it has put a safe distance between the visitor and itself, down it drops into the
marsh again and is gone. The blackbirds themselves
are no more astonished at me than I am always at
the bittern. I think it inhabits this world by accident.

The great blue herons have become much com-
moner today. They traverse the marsh, back and
forth, in direct lines of flight, as if on errands, beating
their wings easily and trailing their legs. Though the
wood ducks are common in the inlets, today all but
one are drakes. The nesting season must have begun,
and the females are in confinement, attending to their
eggs.

It was another mundane day by the time I left Dyke,
beautiful but not miraculous; not a cloud to be
seen in the blue sky, and no haze left among the trees.
The world had a certain assurance now, it was well
established, it had begun to forget its beginnings. The

birds sang less frequently and went about their business. It seemed a long time, pedaling along the road, since I had flown through the clouds. I weighed the evidence of my eyes critically now, and made scientific notes in my mind. It was a beautiful day. All the trees were in foliage; but for the most part it was not full foliage, the leaves had not attained their final size. The change from day to day was harder to see now, for, while the rate of growth may have remained constant, as the leaves became larger their relative increase became less and the daily development, therefore, less conspicuous.

The delicate wild flowers of spring were everywhere, and though the redbud was past its prime, the lilacs and azaleas, the dogwood, and the little violets in the shadows and among the roots of the trees were flourishing as ever. The dogwood, in its fullest bloom, was like magic. Peering deep into the woods, you did not see the tree at all, but only the spatter of white petals suspended in the gloom. Everywhere in the darkness you saw these spatters of dogwood. For the first time this week the honeysuckle that blankets the ground had become alive. It was again green and growing in its profusion. Its old tentacles were interlaced and matted, but their new tips reached upward, climbing into the shrubs and intertwining themselves about the trunks of trees. The leaves that had been furled and brittle last week were now soft, green and virginal, opening out and relaxing. The honeysuckle was as if newly filled with its original aspiration of increase. Last week it had been old and this week it was born again. It was already passionate. It was on the verge of becoming riotous and luxuriant.

In one of his essays T. S. Eliot has written that the statement "Beauty is truth, truth beauty . . ." means nothing to him—"and the reason must be either that I fail to understand it, or that it is a statement which is untrue." I know that difficulty well, recalling how I used privately to puzzle over this line. I was a school-boy then, at that age when one is forever straining against the boundaries of one's mind to discover some final statement of the nature of things. What could Keats have possibly meant by that assertion, which all the pedants repeated as if its meaning was quite obvious, and quite obviously sublime? Why should a thing be true simply because it was beautiful, or beautiful because it was true? It was one of those statements, such as the Bible is full of, that made me feel I was not a bright boy, while they also aroused, as an alternative, the suspicion that literature was a hoax. I am glad I did not settle for the suspicion, seeing how the world suffers from those who, for their pride's sake, destroy what they do not understand. Had I taken that course I might have earned popularity as a nihilist by assuring my fellow blindmen that there was no light. How eagerly we acclaim those who tell us that everything which has been called good is fraud or illusion! It relieves us of any need to be humble.

The years have passed, and today Keats's statement is no longer in the list of pronouncements that puzzle me. It fits the world I have learned to see. Man's spirit dwells in this world as in exile, wandering restlessly about in it like a victim of amnesia, searching endlessly for a home it cannot remember. There is, perhaps, just enough instinctive recollection to tell it when the search is warm, when cold. In the midst of what is fluid and formless, it seeks form and solidity; in the midst of change it seeks the immutable. We men are like those marine organisms that drift helplessly in the currents and washings of the ocean until they can find some ledge of solid rock or sunken wreck to which to attach themselves, when they begin to grow and multiply. We live to no purpose until we attach ourselves to reality. But such is the turbulence of this oceanic world that we are repeatedly swept off soundings, repeatedly compelled to find them anew.

In this quest for something lost, for the ideal and immutable nature, the eternal reality, whatever reminds us of it or at least suggests it to us is beautiful. The latest movie or the latest novel may for the moment distract me from that quest, but it does not satisfy me because it is not real. The search is still to be made, and I must make it or quickly seek some new distraction. It is different when I come upon a book or a poem or a piece of music, or a direct experience of the world, that heightens the world's reality and gives me a solider footing in it. A fairy tale may do it, or the legend of Genesis, better than the most scrupulously factual report on the unreal world in which most of us live. Do not tell me that a play or a novel is bad because it does not show people behaving as, in fact, they do behave. It may show them behaving precisely as they do behave, and still be untrue if their lives are untrue. The characters in *Macbeth* discuss their affairs in blank verse with ghosts and demons, yet I find the true world in *Macbeth* where I do not find it in my daily newspaper. The senator orating on Capitol Hill is a sham and a grotesque illusion next to the Thane of Glamis. He does not really exist, as you will see for yourself when he dies and reality is no less for his passing. He is like the mystery novel that you throw away when you have finished it, or yesterday's newspaper. I doubt not that he once had the chance to be real, but he lost it by indulging himself in the distraction of his own oratory.

What we truly call truth is what reveals to us that ideal and immutable reality toward which our lost souls grope. What we truly call beautiful is what gives us that satisfaction. The Hermes of Praxiteles is beautiful, where the paunchy politician is not, because the one represents man truly while the other is a gross distortion, like the reflection in a warped mirror. The one is man, the other is an aberration.

I come to the conclusion that only nature in its pure form is absolutely beautiful, that any distortion of nature lessens its beauty by so much. The form of an airplane is beautiful to the extent that its lines, like those of a bird, are imposed by the natural element through which it moves. It is beautiful in that it expresses the nature of air, revealing natural laws. Music is beautiful when it epitomizes the rhythms that are characteristic of everything in nature, the beating of a bird's wings and the beating of my heart, breathing, the alternation of the day and night, the phases of the moon, the life cycle, the constant revolution of the seasons. We are comforted by what is eternal.

I wonder that there has been so little comment among us on the fact that nature is invariably beautiful. Perhaps it is because, in our generation, we have become so isolated from the natural world that, if we appreciate what is beautiful at all, we appreciate it as art, at second hand. We do not know the source itself, with which art connects us. In the same fashion I might fail to recognize the electric light by which I work in my seclusion as the light of the sun itself, allowing myself to think that the glass bulb and the connecting wire have some intrinsic energy of light. Another way to say that beauty is truth is to say that art is nature. Art makes nature comprehensible by reducing it to the scope of our vision. It interprets between man and the infinite. It gives us a sense of what might otherwise escape us altogether by its vastness and prolixity.

I cannot understand the pedant or the intellectual who claims to find beauty in the poetry of Walt Whitman, but is unmoved by the repeated roar of the surf washing the length of the shingle, or the phrases of a thrush singing. I hold him suspect. Like as not you will find him praising the poetry for its dross, confusing the poet with the pamphleteer, as if the subject of poetry were politics. I never read a poem on political science, or saw the oil painting of a political theory. The intellectual who praises Shelley's poetry for the socialism he associates with it is akin to the old Scotchman who ordered his portrait painted with an expression of unalterable opposition to the established church. Whatever is beyond nature is also beyond art. Whatever is unreal is unfit for art.

We men may compare ourselves to those coral organisms that affix themselves, generation after generation, atop the remains of their ancestors, thus building upward so that someday their descendants, if not themselves, will reach the celestial light above the surface of the sea. But the storms of the ocean depths are forever tearing loose the structures so painfully built, setting new generations adrift. The work of centuries is dissipated in one cataclysmic night. New structures then have to be built all over again, generation by generation, on what remains of the old. Given such a fate, what nobler mission is there for a man than to leave his skeleton on the highest ledge he can find while yet he lives? Death is truly terrible only for him who at last sinks alone to the darkness and cold of the ocean bottom.

In itself, death, like birth, like the endless succession of nights upon days, is beautiful because it is real. There is something you can hold to. Death implies birth as birth implies death; it completes the greatest paradox, that of the mortality of the individual and the immortality of species. It has its place in the rhythm of nature. A man who outlives the normal span of existence becomes steadily uglier until he is

repulsive. My knowledge that the sun will set saddens
me as I watch it rise, but certainly makes the dawn
no less beautiful. Without that knowledge, perhaps I
should not get up to see it at all. With the lady who
said she accepted the universe, whatever else I may
do I am sure I had better reconcile myself to reality.
I had better come to terms with truth. It will not come
to terms with me, and I shall not find beauty elsewhere.

When you have been out before dawn, when you have
flown through clouds and primordial mists, when
you have seen the earth created and have relived Genesis, when you have struggled through the primeval
wilderness, when you have bicycled fifty miles and
returned in the afternoon to the camp of man, you
must be prepared to accept the sunset. The day is
closing down. It makes no difference now whether the
hopes of Paradise were realized or not. The world has
grown old and is tired. Now the sinking sun has fallen
behind the trees across the street; it is dusk; the world
is fading out. At last there is only the "huge and
thoughtful night." One wonders, does God still dwell
in the tents of Shem in the darkness, or is this but the
memory of an illusion? Soon there is only sleep. The
cycle of existence is over.

In crossing April 8 off your calendar, you cross out
spring and summer and autumn, the life of man, and
the history of the world.

———

In East Potomac Park, at one point in the two miles
of otherwise unbroken greensward, there was in the
spring of 1945 a shallow excavation, perhaps a hun-

dred yards long, where topsoil had been removed for use elsewhere. This was another breach, like the crack in the pavement of the parkway, through which the wilderness entered. Rain water had collected in it, and a few clumps of marsh grass—of what origin, God

knows—had already grown up among the tumbled clods left by the workmen's shovels. Mixed flocks of greater and lesser yellowlegs now frequented it, wading in the shallow water, poking their bills here and there. The migrating swallows dipped down to it as they passed. Ring-billed gulls congregated in it to rest and preen. Killdeer and spotted sandpipers walked up and down over the clods. It was the only place in the city where I ever saw least sandpipers. One morning I found a pair of blue-winged teal sitting together on a clod in the new sunlight, busy with their bills among their feathers, combing them out smooth.

One would think the municipal authorities might have put a fence about this minuscule wilderness and directed tourists to it. After all, they provide for an excellent zoo in Rock Creek Park where citizens may go to gaze upon the creatures of the wilderness, teal and geese and pintails swimming about the duck-pond, silver gulls from Australia in one cage, night herons in another, eagles and turkey vultures in another. If these prisoners are an attraction, how much more so their wild progenitors!

There is, however, an essential difference. The caged birds in the zoo are no longer the creations of nature but the creatures of man. They represent his conquest and lordship, as does the internal-combustion engine. This is what their display means. For a like purpose, Vercingetorix was paraded through the streets of Rome by Julius Caesar. The little shop-keeper on his Sunday outing would rather gaze upon the captured lion pacing behind bars than upon his unconquered brother of the wilderness, not only because he feels more secure but because he feels more important. The little shopkeeper delights to hear the great lion roar, knowing that it is helpless before him. His stature is again increased when he watches the wild geese in the duckpond, brought low by him, their wings cut, scrambling for the bread crumbs he throws them. This world is never so much man's world as at the zoo.

What else but this same need to glorify himself impels a man to boast of the wingspread of the hawk he has shot, and to have it mounted for display? Men cannot endure the wilderness except as they take satisfaction in reducing it. In Rock Creek Park, when the underbrush has grown dense, the civic authorities employ laborers to clear it out, for no accountable reason except that it pleases them better if the park is less wildly natural, showing plain signs of man's handiwork. I have seen the owner of a country estate walking about his woods, instructing his workmen to cut down this tree and that in order to open them out a bit, surely not because the woods were improved, but because he could not feel himself truly in possession until he had left his mark upon them. He had to establish human mastery.

But this little garden of wilderness that had grown up in the excavation was not of man's planting. The governmental authorities, who are responsible for the upkeep of Potomac Park, had certainly not ordered it. The contrast it presented in its unkempt wildness with the two miles of cultivated lawn that surrounded it must have been a source of uneasiness to them. Every morning now, when I passed, the workmen were backing their dump trucks up to it, filling it in. Day by day, the marsh grass and the ducks and the sandpipers were being crowded out, the frontier was being pushed back. Next spring I shall have to look elsewhere for like signs of the inextinguishable wilderness.

———

Spring was advancing.

In the deepest gloom of the woods, where I often pass when I walk to work, there is a natural amphitheater at the foot of a cliff. It reminds me of a place in the uninhabited rain forest of Central America where, in a darkness like that of the ocean bottom, we rode along the base of a stone escarpment towering above us as far as we could see. So the continental shelf must appear to creatures that creep and crawl on the ocean floor. Standing amid the forest verdure on the brink of this cliff, you are level with the tops

of the trees below. To fly you would only have to lean
forward. Rock Creek is down there below, on the
other side of the glade, where you hear it. This standpoint has a certain grandeur. There is another sort of
grandeur when, at twilight, you look up from the pit
below, the grandeur of the nether world. It is the
place for a nocturnal campfire and, perhaps, conspir-
acy.

A pair of phoebes occupy this amphitheater every
summer, as I think they must have since the days
when even the Indians had not come and this was ut-
termost wilderness for hundreds of miles around.
Phoebes are not such common birds here as farther
north, but they are common enough so that you
would be sure of a pair in spring in a setting like this.

There was great excitement the morning of April
13. One of the phoebes was calling stridently and
continuously,   *wheeby-wheeby-wheeby-wheebily-whee-*

by . . . Following its call, I found it exploring the face of the cliff, hovering before it, fluttering from one narrow ledge to another, trying out all possible landings for possible nesting sites, never still for a moment. Its mate, perched on an open twig, followed its actions attentively but was silent.

The material universe, I am told by the physicists, owes its stability to the balance of dynamically opposed forces. The appearance of inertia in the Rock of Gibraltar is an illusion, like the apparent inertia of two wrestlers locked fast in each other's grip. The stability of the atoms that compose the stone is produced by the unresolved conflict between positive and negative charges of energy evenly matched. In that great molecule which we call the solar system, the earth holds its place only because the centrifugal force to which it is subject is perfectly countered by the opposing force of gravity. We are suspended in space as on tenterhooks.

The principle of balance is equally illustrated by upsets in nature, since every change produces compensating changes, so that the movement of my little finger compels the universe to shift its forces and establish a new balance. If it were not for this compensation I could overthrow creation.

God sent Satan into exile to establish his own kingdom of darkness so that the kingdom of light might exist. He produced good by creating evil. He admitted the agent of Satan into the Garden of Eden because that was the only way to offer man the golden opportunity that man muffed. As any reader of fairy tales knows, there can be no virtue where there is no wickedness. Lancelot, the Ill-Made Knight, is essentially more beautiful than the perfectly made Galahad.

How much the virtue of a benign monarch is enhanced in our eyes if it is said of him, for example, that he had a weakness for women! God himself did not acquire the personal attribute of goodness until he came to earth and personally assumed the original sin. Everywhere we turn in this world we see this same principle of balance between opposites. There is no light without darkness, no heat without cold, no health without sickness, no life without death, no liberty without law, no growth without decay, no attraction without repulsion, no positive without negative, no virtue without vice, no masculine without feminine, no love without hate, no truth without falsehood, no reality without illusion. The water is wet to us who know dryness, but not to the fish. Night itself could not exist until God had divided the day from it.

Everywhere there is this balance of opposed principles, and endless compensation for changes. You may depend upon it that as soon as peace ever comes to the earth a generation will arise to glorify war and combat. When we have perfect liberty we shall be ready to give it up. If it were not for this principle, history would cease; because of it we must revise our conventional ideas of heaven. We look to the darkness for the sunrise, and we have winter to thank for spring.

———

I quote here a passage from Conrad's *Lord Jim*. It is Stein ("He was . . . a naturalist of some distinction, or perhaps I should say a learned collector")—it is Stein commenting on a rare butterfly in his collection:

" 'Marvellous!' he repeated, looking up at me. 'Look! The beauty—but that is nothing—look at the accuracy, the harmony. And so fragile! And so strong! And so exact! This is Nature—the balance of colossal forces. Every star is so—and every blade of grass stands *so*—and the mighty Kosmos in perfect equilibrium produces—this. This wonder; this masterpiece of Nature—the great artist.' "

If spring means the coming of summer, it likewise represents the fading of winter. It is a passing away. There are spring departures as well as arrivals. The juncos, the tree sparrows, the pintails, the beautiful drake mergansers of both species (American and red-breasted) are already gone. Of the thousands of gulls only a few immature birds remain to roost on the railings at Hains Point. The end of winter comes now, in the second half of April. Until now the world has been still a candid world; still an open, geometrical world; a world of mechanical distances and space. Nothing has stood between me and the line of the horizon, my eyes focused on perspectives leading in every direction to infinity. This world has been occupied, for the most part, by large birds of ranging and powerful flight, by gulls and ducks, eagles, hawks, vultures. Now the verdure of summer is closing in like a fog, and the great fowl are departing. The bright and candid Arabian desert becomes a shut-in Amazonian forest. The focus of attention shifts from the exposed stretches of river and marsh to the shadowy enclosures; from the aeronauts of the open to the swarms of small birds that are known as voices more often than forms in the foliage, among the confusing lights and shadows—scratching perhaps in the leaves, near but out of sight, or releasing their songs from stations in the tangle overhead. The game here is not so much to follow them as to remain motionless, a

shade among shadows, until they show themselves—
it may be for one sparkling moment on a twig in a
thread of sunlight, or darting from cover to cover. I
shall no longer need my bicycle, as before, to project
myself through space like the long-winged flyers. I,
too, change with the season, suiting myself to it. Like
the creatures of the summer woods I become adept at
concealment and quiet, moving in short stages from
cover to cover. My very thoughts, bold and free-rang-
ing before, become occult and dappled.

I say this is imminent. It is now the end of winter.
Before it passes altogether (though it will never pass
altogether) I shall have another few days on the river
observing the waterfowl, late transients for the most
part, not resting at their leisure for weeks on end, but
pressing north.

———————————

It is Saturday, April 14. The death of a leader has led
the government to close its tiers of cells, in the afternoon, and turn us loose. The funeral is to take place.
Death is in everyone's mind; there is a pervasive common feeling, not of sadness but of desolation. Not be-
reavement but the consciousness of time and change
oppresses the crowd, gives it pause, confuses it for the
moment as a swarm of ants is confused by the cata-
clysm of a human footfall. Nature has asserted its
superiority to politics. We are confronted with the
majesty of a truth, which has come upon us by surprise. Through a rent in the veil of illusion we see,
involuntarily, beyond the present. In this moment before the breach closes, we cannot help but see how
even the greatest among us is still subject to the same
cycle of life as the fish in the pond or the flower in
the sand. The event touches us all, for the moment,

with the sense of all things passing. *Hic jacet* mankind.

What have they done to him who was our leader,
where have they taken him . . . ? The question
is mocked by a silence, a universal quiet, not to be
endured by men of action. Has not medical science
allowed nature to flout most grave considerations of
human policy? On Capitol Hill there is talk of an official investigation. And so the veil of illusion is repaired, life in the hive returns to normal.

Every day has its passing, and every season. One
need not follow a cortege for the taste of death. In the
afternoon Og and I are off by bicycle upon the trail of
another funeral. The morning had been warm and
windless, the sun burning through a haze. At noon-
day the sky had altered: storm clouds gathered overhead, the world grew dark, the wind rose, the rain at
last came lashing and sweeping in white torrents over
the landscape. . . . We waited out the storm under
the canopy before the airport building, leaning on our
bicycles; then set forth into a washed and dripping
world. The wind blew gustily now, the clouds passed
overhead in confusion. It seemed that winter, utterly
routed in the morning, was making its last unavailing
and convulsive effort to return.

The afternoon was what the weather prophets call
"changeable," as if the weather or the world itself was
ever anything else. It is changeability alone that jus-
tifies the weatherman, the artist, the historian. Like a
passenger on the observation platform of a speeding
train, I watch the present dwindling and disappearing
down the tracks behind, crying with Faust: "Ah, stay,
thou art so fair!" Out of the distance, two thousand
years back, yet as clear as if it were spoken here, the
oracular voice of a philosopher answers me: *"Ars
longa, vita brevis."* (Now is not this the most wonder-

ful form of communication, more miraculous than radio, that enables me to hear the voice of one who has been dead two thousand years?)

Any moment and any scene, if you take your stand upon it, represents the culmination of universal history, its Grand Finale, the ultimate point upon which all lines of development converge. I am conscious of this as I stand upon this ground, and of my immeasurable responsibility. It rests with me whether universal history was all for nothing. On this ground, as on every beach and bank, I confront Proteus, the ancient one of the sea, whose speech is sooth if he will only speak, but whose form is changeful and elusive. I must grasp him steadfastly and press him, though he assume the shapes of wild beasts or running water, until at last in his proper shape he stands before me to be questioned. I hold this afternoon of April 14, this scene of clouds and wind and ducks on the river, in trust. There will be other afternoons and other scenes going by, but this one never again.

Even in the city, on such an afternoon as this, men cast questioning eyes at the sky. Racks of clouds assemble against the sun, moving fast, and disperse again. The horizon is murky here, clear there. The earth is light and gloomy by alternate fits. Now the atmosphere is sultry, as if the storm had passed without effect; again a wind comes running along the ways and it is chilly. The river is ruffled here by gusts, roughed up for the moment over a large area, while elsewhere it still mirrors the uncertain sky. At last, as the afternoon lengthens, the uncertainty is resolved. The wind comes cool and steady from the northwest, the clouds travel in one direction overhead across the long reach from horizon to horizon. . . .

The river just off the large inlet at Dyke is the principal station for transient ducks. There are lines and little rafts of them out there, bobbing in the waves, sparkling as the sunlight catches them. Og and I step over driftwood and the exposed roots of trees, through shallow water licking and lapping against the bar, among stones and hummocks, for a closer view. It

is tantalizing to see them away out there, not close enough to identify some of them surely, though close enough to be almost sure that those six in file on the right are old squaws, a salt-water species never seen here by us before. The birds are dancing on the surface with the dancing waves, their forms half hidden from moment to moment in the troughs. At last we have made our way as far as we can without swimming (the tide is in), almost to the outermost point, and there is no doubt left about the old squaws.

Since we saw more species of ducks along the river today than any other day this spring, I list them here so that the matter may stand on record. Off the point at Dyke there were black duck, scaup, goldeneye, old

squaw, ruddy duck, and American merganser; in the marshes, mallard, black duck, baldpate, blue-winged teal, and wood duck; there were green-winged teal at Four Mile Run, and a red-breasted merganser at Roaches Run.

An American eagle, with the white head and tail of the adult plumage, was coming and going all this while over the marshes, circling, careening downwind, beating back against it with powerful wings. Far out on the river, beyond the ducks, a solitary loon flew close over the surface—all length in body and wing, pointed like an arrow—and finally put down with a splashing skid on the water. This river belongs to the loon by an immemorial sovereignty, so that wherever it swims is still wilderness. It purifies the water by its presence.

The ospreys have arrived. One was hanging motionless, flashing its crooked wings, over the lagoon at Roaches Run, looking for some fish below to justify a plunge. Three others are out here at Dyke, diminished by having to share the same sky with an eagle and turkey vultures. Here one hangs in suspension on the wind, moving its wings like a swimmer treading water, falls off on one wing and comes sweeping downwind to a new station where, facing back into the wind, it again hangs suspended, working its wings and concentrating on the water below. Now it collapses, falls like a rock, splashes, and after an instant struggles up from the river with a fish in its talons, pausing just once to shake itself in the air like a wet dog. I am assured that the osprey has been practicing these fine maneuvers for at least two thousand years, since Pliny the Elder wrote: "The osprey remains itself aloft when it spies fishes in the sea below, then dashes headlong on them and secures them, the waters being parted by its breast." Wrapped in his toga, I suppose, Pliny stood on the banks at Ostia and saw this spectacle, just what I see here.

It is not really winter, for all this bluster of the north wind. The woods are great with foliage. Locust trees along the road are in flower, long bunches of white bee-bloom. Over the housetops of Alexandria in the evening the first chimney swifts are coursing and chippering, fresh from the Amazon Valley with perhaps some Amazonian atmosphere still clinging to their wings. I think I sniff its sultry fragrance amid the blowing smoke of the town. The capriciousness of the weather makes no difference to the progress of eternity, which is irremediable. It is too late to save the day. Already the season is older, and mankind. The entire vast universe, a prisoner to time like myself, moves on to April 15.

———————————

To the casual observer, Sunday, April 15, marked no advance in the season. It was a chilly, wet, uniformly gray day. The dampness took the form sometimes of a cold mist and again of a cold drizzle. The observer might have pointed to the ground lost since the ides of March, a month ago, when the heat, reaching 86° Fahrenheit on March 16, had fairly baked the city, driving the citizens out of doors in their shirt sleeves. Fifty-seven degrees was as high as it got today, and the majority of citizens remained indoors. But Og and I were bent on witnessing eternity, and this was part of its progress. The passing season may be likened to a ship, that sometimes runs free before a fair wind, but still moves forward on its course, close hauled, when the wind is ahead. Every day marks an irrevocable advance.

This was the day of the loons. The loons are waterproof and, I think, weatherproof. They represent the primitive reality of life better than men or starlings, having been on earth so much longer. We must take this ancient stability and endurance into account in judging reality. We learn to know a man by the color of his eyes, which is always the same, not by the color of his nose, which changes with the weather. An objective history of life, following this principle, could better overlook all other birds in North America, since none is so primitive as the loon.

The wildness of the loon, however, is not dependent on antiquity. It is a wildness uncontaminated by human associations. The pintail and mallard are responsive to man, willing to make terms with him. The nominally wild ducks wintering at Roaches Run follow you for bread crumbs, while their progeny thrive in zoo or barnyard. I know of no inducements one can offer the loon, or even how one would enter into negotiation with it. It submerges at man's approach and swims away underwater, granting him this much recognition and no more. It makes a fool of him by the ease with which it keeps its distance, and there you have the whole of the relationship. The man gives up at last and the loon continues about its business.

The loon is a bird of solitary passion. The Viking adventurers of a thousand years ago, abroad in their ships on the fog-shrouded waters of the North Atlantic, perhaps lost and blindly drifting, must have shuddered to hear its barking laughter from the surrounding obscurity. The endless murmur and slip-slap of the waves against the hull, the stillness, the wet mist, and suddenly the prolonged peal of laughter from an unseen creature at home in this wilderness—it must have chilled the heart of many a blond warrior. At other times they saw the bird that cried so strangely, a silhouette in the middle distance on still or softly swelling waters; a moment later, however, there was nothing there, and when the "looning" broke out again it was from another quarter and they turned to see the silhouette on the other side. This was no welcome sight to them, like that of the gulls in company dipping from the sky to hover in their wake, being so dissociated from anything human.

I have seen the loon at sea in a cold gale, riding the crested waves as though they were cradling billows, or dipping into the advancing flank of a wave, which rolled past and left no sign that any creature was ever there. To most of us, however, the loon is best known in association with another kind of wilderness. When summer approaches, it resorts for breeding to wooded lakes in New England and Canada, where campers hear its call at night coming over the water. Thoreau in a boat on Walden Pond tried to make its closer acquaintance, but it would have none of him. During the seasons of migration the loon may often be seen in flight where you would never see it otherwise, even over cities, since it must go overland to its lakes in the interior and, when its breeding is over, back to sea. In flight it is unique, its wings slender and flexible by comparison with those of geese. What chiefly distinguishes its rangy silhouette against the sky, however, is its length trailing behind. It does not take off easily, but must scud along the surface, laboring with wings and feet, its rump still splashing and bouncing, before it is free and rises into the air. It is too great a bird to flit from the water. But it can vanish below the surface by merely flicking itself out of sight, and stay under until you give up waiting for its return.

The loon has a monolithic appearance on the water, its silhouette shaped and smoothed out and worn away as if by all the hundreds of thousands of years it has been exposed to wind and weather. It fits into the water and blends to the surface more smoothly than any duck. The body in silhouette is low, long and flat, tapering to the waterline from front to back, and the large, long head with the thick neck rests solidly upon it. Some grebes and ducks ride so high you might imagine them upset by a sudden wave and lying on their sides, but the loon seems to have its center of gravity securely below the waterline. Wild as the loon is, it wears formal black-and-white in the breeding season. It is a solid and also an elegant fowl.

March 31 I had seen the first loon fly north past the Capitol dome. April 14 a single loon landed in the river off Dyke. Today we counted a possible eighteen: a flock of six resting in the river above Mount Vernon, some ruddy ducks nearby; as we watched them, four more passed overhead flying north; returning from Mount Vernon, we found ten in the river where six had been, and four more off Dyke. This was a concentration of loons, for they tend to be solitary. Og reported eight loons flying north next day, April 16. On April 21 one was floating plunk in the middle of the Tidal Basin, in the civilized city of Washington, still wearing its winter plumage.

I have dwelt thus at length on the loon because it represents the world in its sound essence, in its breadth and in its long history, so much better than the worldly lady who, to increase her worldliness, visits the Capitol to take notes on the manners of congressmen—while overhead the solitary loon flies north. Who will establish some correspondence, in this one world of ours, between the lady and the loon?

It is as well not to have too much of a good thing. Anything loses virtue when it becomes ordinary. I have already mentioned the difficulty I have in reconciling the concept of heaven, where there is no darkness or evil, with the possibilities of human experience. There would have to be provision for spending, say, one day each week in hell. Likewise, the absolutely healthy are not so much to be envied as those of us who suffer occasional ill-health. I go through illness like a snake changing its skin, and emerge as if reborn. The world is never more fresh, more buoyant and glorious, than in convalescence, when I am purified.

An appreciation of nature is the proper expression of our urban civilization. The savage does not glory in the wilderness as does the city dweller. Thoreau never acknowledged what Walden owed to Concord, though everything that Walden meant to him implied the imminence of Concord. If it were not for Washington and New York, I would take the wilderness for granted. I thank God that, having discovered the wilderness, I do not take New York and Washington for granted. New York and Washington are merely the walls without which you have no window. I would have them serve no better purpose than to direct the attention of men outward to the world of nature, to be the shadows that frame the sunlight.

Six days a week I had immense satisfaction in escaping from the hive at dawn. Monday mornings I generally got as much enjoyment from doing nothing of the sort. I would be leisurely and luxurious, relaxing my muscles and not opening my eyes more than would serve for a general impression of surroundings, after the full long day given to inspecting the river, the woods, and the marshes. There is a time for action and a time for sloth, a time for alertness and a time for dullness. Indeed, Sunday's cup would perhaps brim too full and the spigot need to be shut off for a day. There is a time for nothing, a time for the commonplace.

It is a sound rule of life to let no rule become invariable. If I ever find myself practicing virtue with constancy, I shall surrender myself to vice for my own salvation, and enjoy it with an appetite long lost by the vicious, until I again have a stomach for virtue. The young men who swing Indian clubs about their heads seven days a week are as much in error as those who lie constantly in the stews. Let there be a balance and an unresolved conflict in all things, until the grave puts an end to it. To do otherwise is to anticipate the grave.

So much for Monday, April 16.

———————

Man's sanity and his deepest satisfaction come from the occurrence of the expected. It is immensely gratifying to know for sure that the sun will set this evening and rise tomorrow. The four seasons are alike beautiful because they come surely as expected, and therefore inform us of an immutable order on which we can depend. The same satisfaction is in the spectacle of the waves advancing and expending themselves on the shore. What horror of mind we should suffer if, watching the waves, we saw them turn back upon themselves and move out to sea! With what anxiety we should watch the sun if there were reason to believe it might stop or return upon its course! It is the certitude of order that enables us to enjoy sanity. Loose your hold on that, and you are plunged into nightmare. You have lost touch with reality.

There is a great deal more insanity within the artificial confines of the hive that we commonly recognize. The sane are, perhaps, in the minority; and at that are likely to be sane only in a relative and negative way, thanks to the dullness of their faculties. You can recognize insanity in a man or in a tiger behind bars, but not in an earthworm. The insane do not necessarily foam at the mouth, or look at you through their fingers. They simply live in a world of their own imagining, and within its terms may be plausible. The insanity may be conspicuous when, in a dance hall at night, you see an adult man with a baton in his hand shaking in a sort of imbecilic trance, eyes closed and head rolling, to the rhythmic din and clatter of an instrumental band. The contents of his mind, if you could open and look into it, would certainly reflect no enduring reality in the world. The insanity is hardly less among urban intellectuals who, artificially secluded from the real world, are preoccupied with structures of thought erected entirely upon the premises provided by their transitory environments. The universe is obviously square to the man who has never ventured out of the square chamber in which he was born. The clerk of the hive who has devoted his life to applying departmental regulations comes to regard those regulations as the expression of a fixed and inviolable order.

To bring order out of chaos is the noblest function of man. I am told that the most backward savages, if you show them a photograph, will see in it nothing but a flat sheet indiscriminately blotched with shades of gray. They recognize no correspondence to three-dimensional reality. So the visual world itself must seem to the infant when first it opens its eyes. Observe its delight, however, when it reaches out its hand to discover that this area of brightness it sees before it is its own foot. Here begins the process of establishing order. The recognition of reality is the source of constant delight and the foundation of sanity. Now suppose that, having learned to identify a certain image as its own foot, the infant should reach out to it and find something else! This is the horror that threatens mankind; this is chaos. To guard against it we must be always extending the area of order that surrounds us and putting the reality we have already discovered to the test. The child reaches out again and again to touch its foot and reassure itself. The man who has learned to read a picture or a book intelligently has further reduced the area of chaos and increased the sources of his assurance. Reality is the more real to him, sanity the more secure. Every real spectacle, every real experience, brings the delight of intelligent recognition. I delight in the drawing Lee Jaques has made of a merganser or the account Pliny has given of an osprey because it confirms my own observation.

But how if my sanity is dependent upon the provisions made by the municipality of Washington rather than upon the order of nature? May I place the same trust in the Potomac Electric Power Company that I do in the sun? Can I be as sure of the plaster ceiling as of the sky? Even though the electric-light switch never fails me and the ceiling never falls, what a piqued and petty semblance of reality this is in which I live! I am the most trammeled of all prisoners because I cannot venture twenty feet from my cell without encountering chaos. I am the most insecure of mortals because I have placed my trust in the perishable works of man. I am the most foolish of thinkers because I have mistaken the conditions of my fabricated world for the terms of nature. Though I do not live long enough to be disillusioned, I will contribute nothing to the enlightenment of mankind but something, perhaps, to its confusion.

I must have not only the security but the freedom that comes with knowledge of the great world. I must have the power to range a thousand years back or forward and be at home all the way, recognizing the same elements of reality that I acknowledge here today. Having discovered the sun, I will not draw back from the past as a time of darkness because it lacks electric light. I will roam over vast extensions of time and space without encountering chaos. Through literature and art I will receive reports of reality from men who, though five thousand years dead or five thousand miles distant, have had the same experience of it as I and tell me so. Knowledge of Washington in the twentieth century gives me the freedom of the city; but knowledge of spring gives me the freedom of the world.

The infant reaches out to test the reality of its foot and is delighted at the confirmation. The rising of the sun gives me a like satisfaction, though it is so frequent and regular that I am in no distress if, sleeping late one particular morning, I fail to see it. I sleep serene and undoubting, having been reassured so often and so recently. The annual recurrence of spring is another matter. In the course of a year my memory has grown less sure. There is increasing suspense, and finally a keener satisfaction at the renewal of the experience. In early March I look at the apparently lifeless skeletons of the elm trees on the Ellipse and say to myself that in two weeks they will be flowering, as the trees have flowered here for a hundred thousand years. In the middle of April I say that in another ten days the city will be full of singing wood thrushes, though there is none here yet. I know all this will be, but it seems to me so miraculous that I cannot take it for granted. I cannot say: Of course! When the first wood thrush does arrive, as predicted, and I hear it singing across the street as I wake up in the morning, I am filled with unutterable astonishment and delight. Bravo the wood thrush! O immutable world, that goes on and on in spite of all the disorder that man engenders within the sphere of his own confinement!

———————

Spring returns year after year, yet "age cannot wither her, nor custom stale her infinite variety." To the fulfillment of one's expectations she is forever adding the joy of the unexpected—like the sea "in no wonder the same . . . and the same in each wonder." Who knows what garment she will wear today or how her hair will be done up; whether she will advance with song and splendor or slip quietly in? I can predict the hour and the minute when the sun will cross the equator, but not the exact day of the wood thrush. I can foretell many of the birds that will be on the list of visitors, but not all—and among them will be some it never occurred to me I might see. I set out each morning not knowing what surprise and new delight may be in store for me.

Among the birds one awaits with suspense every spring are the sharp little terns, relatives of the gulls, the "sea swallows" as they are sometimes called. They are all elegance and deftness, their pointed wings raking back, their tails forked, flicking over the river with bills pointed downward, occasionally diving like arrows into the water, to emerge often with a silver fishling, still thrashing, held crosswise in the bill.

I say the terns are smaller than the gulls, and so they are. But truth is great and has room for exception. The Bonaparte's gull, smallest of New World gulls, is about the size of a typical tern. The Caspian tern, largest of all terns and occurring in scattered locations around this aquaterrestrial globe, is virtually as large as a herring gull and is thus a prodigy in its

own family. I had seen Caspian terns only once, a
small flock that roosted on a mangrove key in the Gulf
of Honduras one night when I was lying off in a small
boat. But that is far away and long ago. . . .

It had been raining when I left home the morning
of April 17. The sky was overcast and a heavy south
wind was blowing warm and damp. Off East Potomac
Park, two Bonaparte's gulls were flying away from me,
flicking low over the water, showing the white flashes
in their wings. It was hard going against the south
wind until I rounded the Point. As I did so, four
pearly sea birds with wings like ribbons and stout red
bills were beating their way out of the Channel,
coming about the Point against me. I looked once and
again, jumped from my bicycle and raised my binoculars, noting all the features from the red bill to the
charred underwing tips and the pointed length of
wing to make certain of my identification. That was
the second time I had ever seen Caspian terns.

———————

I present here, as background to this account, a piece
on the wood thrush and its kin that I wrote in 1942:

I have long had it in mind to set down some personal observations on the genus *Hylocichla,* which
comprises the five species of spotted thrush inhabiting
the forests of North America. The five species are:
H. mustelina, the wood thrush; *H. guttata,* the hermit thrush; *H. ustulata,* the olive-backed thrush; *H.
minima,* the gray-cheeked thrush; and *H. fuscescens,*
the veery. They are all very similar, and yet distinctive too. All are inhabitants of the heavy shade, the
perpetual golden gloom of the forest. They are at
home in the lowest range of the woods, among the
dead foliage and humus on the ground itself, or in the
foliage of the undergrowth. Several of them prefer

steep and generally damp slopes in the forest with outcrops of moss-stained rock. They belong to this habitat as the violets do, and are as much a part of it. In the East in springtime or summer these recesses of the forest would appear to have lost some natural quality if no *Hylocichla* were present. They are not rare, or even uncommon; they are not, like so many exceptionally distinguished birds, subjects for occasional delight only.

In the most diverse sorts of birds, even barnyard fowl, one sometimes catches a mannerism or appearance of the reptilian. This is especially true of the spotted thrushes, which will at times assume attitudes of motionless alertness remindful of lizards, with which they share a distant common ancestor. Of course they are not really like lizards, but one gets a touch of it occasionally, not only in these attitudes but also in a peculiar appearance or expression about the base of the bill and the eyes. It is such a humorless expression as to be laughable on occasion. You see the same thing in the robin, close to, when he holds up his head intent to catch a sound—something primitive and stolid, even harsh, in the expression of the face.

Above—that is, on the head, back, wings, and upper side of the tail—this genus varies from olive-brown to a richer rusty or cinnamon brown. Underneath it is spotted, darkly in the wood thrush, in the veery only faintly on the throat and upper breast. The tail is quite short and the legs are long, as befits birds that hunt their living on uneven ground. But I have never seen the spotted thrushes scratch, like towhees and fox sparrows. They turn the leaves over, in their foraging, with a quick toss of the bill.

In all the woods of North America there are no singers to compare with these spotted thrushes. The mockingbird, which shuns the woods, compares in technical brilliance, but he does not have a song in the sense that these do. He specializes in notes and variations, in the production of striking and beautiful single tones or phrases, but lacks melody. He arouses delight and astonishment, but the singing of the wood thrush and the hermit thrush and the veery evokes wonder. It is hard to associate it with the mundane world. When one listens to their songs with an attentive spirit, at twilight from the depths of the forest, it seems at times as if one heard something more than a singing bird. This is especially true of the veery, which is a less brilliant singer than either the wood or the hermit thrush, but unearthly.

I have become so fond of hearing the various spotted thrushes that I should miss them acutely if I lived where none occurred. As each winter advances, as the lapse of time since I last saw or heard them increases, as the date for their arrival draws nearer, the suspense of my anticipation mounts steadily. The hermit thrush comes early, and may indeed spend the winter at Pound Ridge, my home near the Connecticut border above New York City. But he is a different bird under these circumstances, when the woods are bare. He is merely another brown winter bird, somewhat resembling the fox sparrow, quite silent except for an occasional *chuck* as he flits to a fallen branch or pokes among last summer's leaves. You would hardly think him capable of song.

The hermit thrush is the only one of the spotted thrushes that winters in the United States. The others spend the winter in Central and South America, the olive-back as far south as Argentina. It is strange that birds of such sheltered habitat should launch themselves overseas twice a year—flying close to the waves, I imagine, so that from a ship at sea the traveler might catch an occasional glimpse of a brown speck fluttering in the trough—and yet survive. Even wood thrushes, boldest of all in our parts, are easily confused and sometimes lose their heads altogether when they find themselves out in the open, away from the shelter of their native trees. . . .

Some commentators feel that the song of the wood thrush is marred, or brought short of perfection, by the light and seemingly impromptu phrases interspersed between the flutelike passages. They feel that these touches are often unmusical and somewhat harsh, and so take away from the perfect music of the flute tones. But to me there is extraordinary interest in these grace notes and trimmings, and a sort of uncanny beauty that is lacking from the purer tone of the main phrases, to which they serve as foils.

The ease and leisure of the wood thrush's song is one of its characteristics. The singer is never shaken

with effort like a house wren. Usually he sits motionless on a branch, at rest. Every few seconds (with the regularity of some marvelous mechanical toy) he lifts his head, opens his bill, and delivers himself of a brief phrase; subsiding then until another phrase has formed and is ready to well up within him. The song is discontinuous and never finished. I like especially the little *hip-hip* with which, like a cheer leader, he usually introduces the principal phrases. These phrases generally consist of three or four flutelike notes bound together. They are followed immediately, as a rule, by a muted trill—then silence. . . .

If you held the stuffed skin of a wood thrush in one hand and that of a veery in the other, you would not see any fundamental difference. They would not be exactly the same shade of brown, the veery would not be so heavily spotted below, the wood thrush would be slightly larger. In life, too, these species resemble each other closely, as do all the spotted thrushes. But there are differences of manner and attitude that are fully as great as those of color and marking—rather greater, in fact. The wood thrush is more stalwart, more excitable, more vocal, and more assertive. At the least alarm it puffs itself up, erects the feathers on top of its head, and utters its loud, ringing alarm notes —*pit-pit-pit*. The veery is silent, elusive, and retiring. It is not so much shy as secretive, and this gives it an air of mystery that the wood thrush lacks. A veery may be quite near you in the woods and you will not notice it at all, where a wood thrush would attract your attention with its bold ways.

The wood thrush, in keeping with its boldness, has accommodated itself to our cities. It is at home now, like the catbird, wherever there are shade trees and shrubbery. But it is the only one of the five. At Pound Ridge the veeries are invariably found in dank places, in the low swampy woods that border the large marshes. In June you can hear them just at dusk calling softly to each other across the marshes. You will not find them, ordinarily, unless you are looking for them, and they are apt to fall silent as you draw near. If they are alarmed at your presence, when you have crept up on them, it may be manifested only by a very soft sound, a sort of *whew*, that you will not hear unless you are very close indeed. It is deceptive, and I have sometimes had to watch the movement of a bird's throat to be sure it was uttering the sound at all. I have never seen a veery puff itself up, spread its chest, so to speak, and raise the feathers of its head like a wood thrush. It remains quiet and inconspicuous, no matter what the motive for alarm.

The song of the veery is a soft and continuous swirling sound that gives the impression of spiraling downward. Commentators are at variance over how it should be rated, and understandably so, for it is not comparable to the song of any other bird. It is not brilliant or spectacular, or notable for range and variety—these being the qualities that are usually dwelt on in thinking of birds as rivaling each other in song. This voice is merely uncanny and unearthly. It has a soft, reedy double tone, such as might conceivably be produced by a violinist drawing his bow across two strings at once; but no mechanical instrument could produce such thin, resonant chords. It has also a windy quality, and perhaps one could give an idea of it by comparing it to the sound produced by blowing across the top of a bottle. The overtone, the resonance, as if the bird carried its own echo within itself, might make one think that the song was actually issuing from inside a bottle. It is a soft, tremulous, utterly ethereal sound, swirling downward and ending, swirling downward and ending again. Heard in the gloom of twilight, back and forth across the marshes, it gives the impression that this is no bird at all but some spirit not to be discovered.

In my experience the season during which the song of the veery may be heard lasts less than a month out of the twelve. Like the wood thrushes, the veeries arrive at Pound Ridge about the first week in May. Then you may hear them calling, but you will not hear them sing. The call may be quite loud and carry far, but it is soft in quality. It is of two syllables that blend into each other, a sort of *weheu*—hence the bird's name. Sometimes you hear only the second syllable, very faintly.

It is close to the middle of May when the veeries begin to sing. Evening after evening, for the next three weeks, you can hear them if you go to the right places. Toward the end, however, the songs become intermittent, the singers no longer persist in them. By the middle of June there are young in the nests and the adults no longer have the leisure to sing, or even to call to each other. You will not hear them again, now, until another spring.

When, in the early winter of 1941-42, I moved to the city of Washington, one of my few regrets was that I should be residing too far south to hear the song of the veery when spring came. Veeries do not breed south of central New Jersey, except in the mountains, and they do not sing except on their breeding grounds. Although my time in Washington was almost wholly occupied with other matters, I did not have to give up my pursuit of birds entirely, for I made it a habit to walk to work every morning through such a lovely bit of woodland as you would not look for in any city park. I had between a mile and two miles of this woodland to traverse, and it contained a greater density and variety of birds than you could find in most of the surrounding country. Even barred owls and black-crowned night herons and broad-winged hawks were present. By the middle of May the wood thrushes were in greater profusion than they ever are at Pound Ridge. They sang from all sides, bounded along the path ahead of me, called *pit-pit* in alarm at my passage. The bobwhites were profuse and vocal. I heard their tense, vibrant whistles incessantly and sometimes saw them moving stealthily through the deep shade of the ground cover. Almost every morning while they were in Washington on their way north I heard the olive-backed thrushes. Their song was soft and vibrant, but without the resonance of the veery's, ascending in a series of musical bounds.

On the night of May 20 it rained heavily, clearing at dawn. The woods were still absorbing the night's rain when I walked down in the morning. The sun was just about to make itself felt. Its rays showed against a woodland mist that remained as an aftermath of the rain, leaving patches and sparkles of light at odd intervals. The world, still so fresh and moist, seemed as though it had just emerged from the chrysalis of an age-old darkness.

At one point a small tributary stream tumbles through a ravine to enter the main creek. Back up the ravine the woods are dense and rise steeply on either hand. It is a place of big trees, many beeches with gnarled roots, tall tulip trees, sycamores, and ponderous oaks, all interlaced above so that you see only bits of sky. A soft golden light suffuses the scene. Although I had passed the entrance to this ravine every morning, I had never entered it. This morning, however, something made me pause in front of it. An Acadian flycatcher was uttering its explosive call at intervals, a pewee was voicing its long-drawn sorrow, and I could hear the perky buzzing of a parula warbler directly overhead. When I listened I could hear many other songs and calls farther off. Something, however, had brought the veery to my mind. I waited a moment, listening intently, heard nothing out of the way, and started forward again. I had to stop a second time. Again, some vibration amid all these voices had put me in mind of a veery. And each time I started forward the impression returned. At last I entered the ravine to investigate.

No sooner had I entered than all doubt vanished. Faint but clear, against the murmuring and buzzing of the woods and the roar of water, it came, the swirling, swirling, tremulous spiral of tone, over and over again. I found the delicate bird at the head of the ravine, singing in the forest mist, amid the long rays of golden light. He was moving from branch to branch, raising his head at intervals and opening his bill to release that lovely series of intertwining and falling phrases.

Morning and evening, after that, I took the path through the ravine, expecting every time that the veery would be gone on his way north. He was always there. As soon as I entered his precincts I would again hear the magic spirals of tone, coming as if from nowhere and permeating the forest. At the end of a week it had become apparent that the veery had taken up his territory far outside the normal breeding range of his species.

On June 1, in the morning, I found two veeries singing on the slopes of the ravine. My veery sang and was answered from close by, again and again. The second song, however, did not have the same quality as the first. It was rapid and perfunctory, lacking the full resonance. Hereafter there were three of us who observed the veeries from day to day, wondering whether we dared hope that they were a true pair and would stay to breed in Washington, so far from their native ground. It was hard to know what we should make of the second singer—perhaps a young male not yet in full voice. None of us could be sure the female of the species ever sang. But there was no doubt that the two birds were occupying one territory: several times we saw them chasing each other in play through the trees.

Occasionally, as the season advanced, we did not find either of the veeries for several days in succession. Their singing became less persistent. After June 15 they were no longer heard at all and, lacking the opportunity to hunt them out in the woods, we did not find a sign of them in the nine days that followed. It seemed likely that they had at last resumed their northward course. After all, the latest date we found on the record for Washington was June 2.

It was June 25, on my way to work, when I again saw one of the veeries. On the 26th, again, I found a veery carrying a caterpillar in its bill, not swallowing it, but retaining it in its bill while it continued to forage among the dead leaves. Then it flew off through the woods and I lost it. I said nothing of this to the others, but the following Sunday morning I put on old clothes and set off, determined to find out if the veeries were nesting or to assure myself that they were not.

I was almost three hours about the business. At long intervals I would come upon one or the other of the pair in some part of the woods, hunting food, sometimes swallowing it, sometimes carrying it in its bill. Always it flew off through the woods and I lost it. I could find no center or focal point of activity. The pair seemed to be ranging the woods indiscriminately and aloof from each other.

For their part, the veeries paid no attention to me. They showed no curiosity or alarm, even when I squeaked with my lips in imitations of ravished nestlings. Those squeaks would sometimes set the woods to ringing with alarm all about me. The wood thrushes would shout at me, the catbirds come mewing, the towhees drag their wings on the ground at my feet; Carolina wrens and house wrens would chatter angrily, even the warblers and titmice would come down from the treetops to see what it was all about. But the veeries remained heedless, and I took this for a sign that they were not nesting and consequently did not share the common motive for alarm.

I had actually given up the hunt and was on my way out of the woods when my eye was again caught by one of the veeries. It had a caterpillar in its bill and was uttering its almost inaudible single note, the faint *whew*. It flew toward some shrubbery on the slope, disappeared, returned without the caterpillar, and hopped in its peculiar bounding way among the dead leaves near the path, searching for another morsel. It found another, flew straight to a low branch, and remained there, watching me, uttering its plaintive note repeatedly. It flew to another branch, waited a moment, still eying me, then dropped to a low tangle of vine-clad shrubbery. I fixed it in my binoculars.

The veery was standing on top of the vine, in the open. As I studied it I noticed a stirring at its feet, there among the vine leaves. The bird dipped its head, then flew. An instant later I was looking straight down upon three half-fledged nestlings in an open cup among the leaves. The sensation that filled me at that moment could not have been more overpowering if I had stepped through the shrubbery to find the end of the rainbow.

At midday, April 16, I went out on the roof of my apartment house to take stock of the world and the weather. A west wind was blowing, lofty thunderheads were moving across the sky, so that the sunlight, breaking out intermittently over the city, was intermittently overcome by traveling cloud shadows. Against this sunny and stormy sky migrating hawks were passing in a steady procession, chiefly broad-winged hawks, but occasionally redtails, ospreys, Cooper's and sharp-shinned hawks, and sparrow hawks. Many were so high they showed only as black flakes circling and drifting across the wind. Others swept low over the city, riding the gusty air currents above the buildings. My binoculars, fixed on hawks overhead, discovered a migrating flock of tree swallows, sparkling against the clouds, so remote that I could not see them with the naked eye. Chimney swifts were migrating too. A couple of killdeer circled between the city below and the clouds above, crying to each other. The local turkey vultures soared lazily, taking their ease, and a sportive flock of pigeons roamed the sky.

The morning of April 17, a green heron took off from a willow on the bank of East Potomac Park, flapped out over the Channel, and returned to another willow farther up. On 17th Street, opposite the Pan American Union, the first yellow warbler of the year sang once—loud, clear, and unmistakable.

I would not willingly give up our four seasons for a Kingdom of Heaven in which the sun shone eternally with equal warmth and light, in which the grass was forever green and the birds sang constantly. I would have no unchanging splendor. Though the violin stopped at the most musical note in the sonata and sustained it indefinitely, I could not sustain it in myself. Let the violin go on and return to that note at judicious intervals, so that I may always hear it afresh. Nothing is precious without a degree of rarity. Be warned that in the land of eternal spring you will find the inhabitants blind and deaf.

This is not to say that we must go through pain in order to enjoy any particular pleasure, though there is undoubtedly truth in this as the world goes. In my Kingdom of Heaven, as I choose to conceive it, enjoyment of life is sustained by the variety and contrast among its pleasures. The Kingdom has, I think, four revolving seasons, each with its own inspiration and delight. They bear a particular resemblance to the seasons in the northeastern United States; for the abundant variety and contrast of climates within this one area in the course of a year is its most notable feature. Where else are the summers so hot and the winters so cold, the springs so fresh and the autumns so mellow? Its separate seasons have so much to offer that the year is hardly long enough to contain them. I have lived in lands that boast an equable climate and found the year wearisome in its length, but here it moves and passes before your senses almost too quickly. In Washington, except for a month or a month and a half in winter, you can see changes in the season from week to week the year around. Often these changes are dramatic in their suddenness, taking place overnight. A wave of migrants, arriving while I slept, have transformed the scene for me since yesterday, and may be gone tomorrow; in two or three days of March the flowering trees have burst into bloom; in a few days of October the foliage has turned yellow and orange, purple and scarlet. I have read accounts of the subdued and gradually changing seasons in England, and I have seen something of the seasons in our own West, and in neither place is there anything as dramatic as this. We have tropical summers and arctic winters; our spring and fall are like nothing else on earth.

The night of April 17 the wind blew from the south. In the crepuscular daybreak of April 18 I awoke to the voice of a whippoorwill across the street: that rapid, vibrant, steady pulsation of sound, like something organic in the earth itself, like the beating of one's own heart. It invested the whole atmosphere, pausing occasionally, then resuming. The robins were already caroling, the cardinals contributing their beads of song to the chorus, which was constantly being swelled by additional voices. Suddenly a new voice came in, and for me a new season, a new life long awaited, had at last begun. It was a wood thrush, uttering the bell-like phrases, the trills and grace notes, that I recalled from other springs. Steadily, steadily it sang, with leisure and confident ease, as if knowing that for all its long absence it belonged on the scene as rightfully as anything else, more rightfully than much else. I had been expecting it and here it was, like the unfailing voice of truth in a world of rumor and delusion.

Whippoorwill and wood thrush had been borne up on the south wind of overnight—and what else? One gets dressed hurriedly, on tiptoe, straining one's ears for every sound from the woods across the street. I am out of doors while there is still a dawnlight and the freshness of dawn in the atmosphere, though the sun has risen clear of the horizon and bathes the earth in brilliant illumination. At the foot of the street, in some garden shrubbery, a catbird is chattering softly and continuously, with whistles and squeaks, recalling all the catbirds of yesteryear, of my almost forgotten life. In the deep woods of Massachusetts Park, where the road winds through them, in the same hollow under the slope where I have heard him each spring, the same individual every year by the cadence of his voice, I hear again the ovenbird, periodically asserting himself, dominating the atmosphere with the crescendo of his song. Other wood thrushes have taken up their stations here and there in the city overnight. There has been a clandestine invasion and occupation while we slept. More parula warblers and black-and-white warblers have arrived, and this morning you hear them everywhere, the wisps of song, the vocal signatures uttered at regular intervals from the trees. This is the news of the day.

Wherever you are in the city now, and at any time of day, you may look up from the streets, like a mouse peering up from its runways in the tall grass, and see the chimney swifts passing overhead. Here is the great world itself within the bounds of my nutshell, and suddenly I "count myself a king of infinite space." That very swift, now veering over the housetops, was lately careening in that same fashion over the forested expanses of the Amazon Basin, sweeping that other sky as now it sweeps this. It is as if I had the power to resolve this globe under my feet like a plaything. All movement is relative, so why may I not say that this very scene, this Washington, is like a ship crowded with humanity that cruises south into the tropics at this time of year, rather than that the warm weather and the luxuriance of flower and foliage and the multitude of summer birds come here to visit? Indeed, these swifts remain fixed with reference to the sun, and it is the world that tilts beneath them. I cannot complain at the sessile existence I am constrained to lead these days, since this continuous change of seasons is travel. Knowing the four seasons, here in Washington, I am more traveled than the swifts, which know hardly more than one.

It is the evening of April 19, the approaching end of a cloudless day. Og and I are free this evening, and there are any number of things we might do: go to the movies, or a concert at Constitution Hall, or whatever is playing at the National Theater. The newspapers list a number of spectacles for which we might buy tickets. They do not list the spectacle we choose, for which no tickets are asked. It takes place toward dusk at the garage behind the Wardman Park Hotel, on Calvert Street. As the hour approaches, you may see the swifts in twos or threes or dozens making for this roosting place across the housetops from all points of the compass. A small, irregular band of them is already wandering about the sky in the vicinity of the garage chimney when we arrive. You can hear their chippering above the noise of traffic in the streets. The band is constantly augmented by new arrivals until it is a mass of little birds streaming overhead, wandering out over the Shoreham Hotel and back again, here and there, growing constantly as the new arrivals join it until you see the full spectacle in its wonder and impressiveness, all the swifts for miles around gathered into a cloud that now begins to take shape. The shape is that of a great wheel revolving above the chimney. As the light fades from the sky, the revolving wheel is tilted obliquely, its lower side just clearing the chimney. Watch as you may, however, you will see no birds enter it yet. Some hesitate briefly as they pass, but are carried on in the stream. I do not know how the signal is finally given, but it is as if a sergeant among them had blown a whistle and cried "Fall in!" Instantly the wheel is broken, one end of it turning straight down into the opening of the chimney. The myriad birds in their formation now resemble a whirlpool of water being sucked into a drain. Within a minute the sky is utterly drained of swifts, and the chorus of chippering has ceased. Good night!

It is, of course, good morning to the black-crowned night herons. From their diurnal roost in Rock Creek Park, now that it is dusk, they are making toward the river to feed. The sky is never empty of them at this hour, or not for long. Singly, or more often in twos and threes, they flap over the city, sometimes wavering and dipping in their flight as if uncertain of their

purpose. Now and again one cries *wok,* an unmusical
cry that I shall hear at night through the open window as I lie in bed. Here is one trying to catch up with
a pair ahead of it, beating its wings willfully and repeating the only sound it knows as often as it has
breath to do so. They disappear, all three, over the
housetops to the southwest.

To Og, who has recently been in India, these birds
flapping slowly across the evening sky are the counterpart of the gigantic Assamese fruit bats, which he
watched at dusk on the way to their feeding grounds,
almost indistinguishable on the wing at a distance.
For the moment, Connecticut Avenue leads to
Dibrugarh.

The passers-by see none of this, though they have
only to lift their eyes from the pavement. This couple
hurrying along the street, the man pulling out his
watch and telling the time to the woman on his arm,
may be on their way to the nearby moving-picture
theater, where they will see a picture showing the
wonders of the wilds of Assam, or perhaps a nesting
colony of black-crowned night herons on the banks of
the Pee Dee River. They have not time to stop and
see these herons passing over their heads and calling
to one another in the dusk.

————————

Men do not commonly see what is before their eyes
or hear what rings in their ears unless it is pointed
out to them in a tone of accepted authority and given
public importance. Let the newspapers announce that
tonight there will be a flight of herons over the city:
the streets and housetops will be thronged long before
dusk with citizens scanning the sky. But unless the
flight is thus accredited it will do no good for me to
stop the passer-by and point it out to him. He will

simply shrug me off and hurry on to the movies, where the professional voice of an announcer assures him, in tones to which he responds, that what he sees is a wonder. I have observed as many as one hundred

and fifty vultures circling low in one flock over Connecticut Avenue when it was crowded with people, and none taking notice. Yet many of these people will go to the zoo to gaze upon the caged turkey vultures.

The other day what was said to be an eagle was publicly reported to have perched on the roof of Mrs. Marie J. Bird's home at 315 Main Street, Port Wash-

ington, Long Island. The result, according to the
New York *Herald Tribune,* was that "so many people gathered in front of Mrs. Bird's home to look at
the roof where the eagle had been that policemen
were sent there to protect her flower beds."

One reason why the ordinary citizen remains un-
mindful of the unannounced vultures and night herons above him is that he was not born with eyes in
the top of his head. Man lives on the ground and has
his living from the ground. His eyes turn down more
easily than up. To his practical mind the sky is nothing, an expanse of emptiness, unfilled space. As such
it does not invite his attention. This reasoning is
borne out, I think, by the fact that in the American
tropics, where these same vultures are common den-
izens of the streets, everybody is aware of them. The
visitor from Washington who lands at, say, Santiago
de Cuba, sees the turkey vultures perched on the eaves
of the houses or walking grotesquely along the pavement, and regards them with interest as exotic and
new to his experience, although he might have seen
them every day in Washington if he had only looked
at them. The explanation is that in Santiago he finds
them descended to the horizontal level of his observation. Likewise, the citizen who never sees the vultures
and the herons against the sky is not unaware of the
"sea gulls" along the waterfront, although they are
no more spectacular. They simply happen to come
within range.

There are, of course, degrees of seeing, and to most
of us adults the world of nature, even when looked at
directly, is seen but obscurely, as if out of the corner
of one's eye. It is seen, in a physical sense, but makes
no impression on the mind. It is "as the cuckoo is in
June, heard, not regarded." That is why it would be
useless for me to point out the herons or the vultures
to the adult passer-by, for though he looked and saw

it would be but blindly. There is an atrophy of the
mind that takes place after childhood. I once labored
assiduously, in the spring, to teach an elderly gentle-
man the simple and distinctive call of the phoebe,
just that one bird call, so that he could recognize it;
but with all the will in the world he was unable to
register it on his mind. The innate eloquence of the
world in which we live, its multifarious and unceas-
ing appeal, induces a protective deafness in men who
are not unlimited in their capacity to respond.

The archangel should be warned that, unless he ar-
ranges for the customary publicity in advance, there
will be few to hear him when his trumpet announces
Judgment Day. Perhaps he is blowing First Call to
Judgment now, and I do not hear him simply because
I have not learned how. I never heard even a wood
thrush until I was a grown man, though I must have
been surrounded by them every spring. Each year I
discover new sights and sounds to teach me how blind
and deaf I must still be.

———

In the veery woods, on April 21, a crested flycatcher,
newly arrived from across the Caribbean, was shout-
ing. I know no other way to describe his familiar call.
Wheeeep! he shouted, for all the world to hear, again
and again. This in itself was the announcement of another spring.

———

If, on a night in spring, the city of Washington should
be silently ringed by flames leaping from the horizon
as in the fire scene of *Die Walküre;* or if the sound of
plucked harp strings should shake the earth on which
it stands; or if rose petals should rain all day in pro-

fusion over it: you would expect the ordinary citizen to notice and be in some way aroused. So it is not surprising that at this time of year he sometimes catches his breath at the sudden beauty of the trees that adorn it. The city is a vast arboretum, at its best in this one moment of the year when so many trees are in flower and the foliage is abundant but still fresh. New Hampshire Avenue, its elms arching to meet in interlacements overhead, is like the nave of a cathedral, filled with the same soft and mottled light. The red-eyed vireos preach continuously along its length to anyone who will pause and hear them. The lindens lining Massachusetts Avenue, which seemed bleak in their nakedness, have suddenly become so many bowers of springtime, each concealing the privacy of its interior. Overlooking it from the hill on which the Cathedral stands, the city appears embowered in woodland, its buildings showing above the green foliage. From the Connecticut Avenue Bridge you look out over a forested valley that might be tributary to the Amazon Basin.

The accession of this summer foliage, which seems now to have been sudden, is more revolutionary than anyone had expected. It is not simply that leaves have come out to adorn the winter skeletons of the trees: the skeletons themselves are now only the half-hidden supports of green canopies, often set in tier above tier, beneath which the earth is shadowed and sheltered. You look into the White House grounds as into chapels inside which the elm boles rise and branch, the light subdued, mysterious, and dappled.

At this time of year the green is fresher and brighter than it will be again. There is more variety to it, from the yellow green of the red oaks and the silver green of the sycamores to the somber green of the beeches against the blue bark. I don't know when the leaves came out on the oak trees—the red oaks,

the white oaks, the pin oaks that line so many streets
—but suddenly they are there, yellow-green and soft
and fresh, as if moist, where later they will be relatively stiff, dry, and dark. At this time of year, too, the
abundant paulownia which no one had noticed before has suddenly become a mass of lavender that
interrupts the green. This is the paulownia season in
Washington. I wonder when it was, and by what de-
cision, that this Asiatic tree was planted so abun-
dantly about the city, in the deep woods and in the
yards and gardens alike. People who never notice
such things now notice the paulownia and ask what
it is. The dogwood is still in bloom, though now it
bears new green leaves along with its white or pink
petals. The locust trees still bear their delicate and
fragrant spires of white bloom amid their fresh foliage.

This is the time when one discovers anew the wonder of standing in the woods. What a profusion of delicate forms surround and enclose one, not only on all
sides but above and below as well! The view in every
direction is not so much shut off as confused and lost
in the variegated lights and shadows. Living creatures
may lurk or move all about, impossible to see because
their individual forms are lost in the multitude. They
are as often disguised as hidden by their surroundings. Sight is baffled by the variety of detail, which
still challenges it on all sides. The lights and shadows,
always shifting if ever so slightly, bewilder and amaze
one's vision, which can hardly mark the quick flight
of a bird across them. Are these the woods in which,
only a few days ago, every tree and shrub, standing
naked, could be counted? It is as if magic had come
back to a world that no longer believed in it.

III

I T BEGAN as a mild day, the sky quite clear and blue, but the wind was from the south. During the morning, as the heat increased, spiderwebs gathered and thickened in the sky, veiling the sun until its diffused glare hurt one's eyes. The afternoon was oppressive. In the evening a thunderstorm broke over the city. Before the rain began the sky had darkened, a premature night had fallen, a wind had come up from the west. Lightning flashed, followed by almighty thunderclaps and a sound of furniture tumbling overhead. Then the darkness was relieved, the sky grew luminous, and in this sinister dawn the rain fell. It lashed the trees across the street, their skirts already blown up by the wind. At the climax, for less than a minute, hailstones the size of garden peas bounded along the pavements. At last the rain changed to moderate and steady; chimney swifts reappeared in the sky.

When I reached the Connecticut Avenue Bridge the rain had already stopped. The watery black clouds were still solid over the sky, except in the west, where a gap had sprung between them and the horizon, showing in its spectacular radiance that the sun had just set. Looking over the sea of wet foliage below, one might have been surveying a virgin forest in the tropics. Thin remnants of cloud, clinging to the trees, might have been either the vaporous aftermath of rain or smoke from an encampment of savages hidden on the forest floor. Night herons were crossing the sky, singly, in twos, or in threes, like birds of the tropical dusk, uttering their explosive squawks. Each bird flies as a fish swims, buoyantly, beating across the sky as if through a denser substance than air, yawing somewhat, often dipping and rising.

Surveying this landscape, it seems a long time since the icy days of late January when a cardinal, calling *cue-cue-cue-cue-cue-cue* from a bare tree, awoke a memory and a hope of spring. Yet that was Washington three months ago, not Asia in the Pleistocene. It is hard to believe what can happen in such a short time. There will be no further changes so vast and dramatic in the remaining six weeks before the last spring migrant departs, leaving Washington to face the full summer. The changes now will be changes in detail. The warblers, for example, have arrived; but there will be several times as many of them in the city in another two weeks, both individuals and species. The woods will just begin to fill up now, not only with warblers but with all the woodland birds. Though the swifts are here, the nighthawks have yet to come from South America to bestride the sky over the city. The flowering season of the trees has arrived; but some kinds are yet to flower. Individual trees will not have their full foliage before the middle of May, though already the woods are well roofed. The honeysuckle is not yet in its bloom and fragrance. The weather will become warmer on the whole. But from now on it is chiefly a matter of seeing the last touches applied to the picture of spring.

When a quarter inch of leaf comes out on a bare tree overnight, the change is conspicuous. When a leaf already six inches long grows another quarter inch, the change is less noticeable. Though the leaf grows at a constant rate, the change is less as time passes in proportion to what has already been accomplished.

Professional psychologists, who are occupied so

largely in devising jargon terms for familiar mental attitudes, have been remiss, it seems to me, in overlooking the unlimited human capacity to take for granted. If only they would call it "morphatic adjustment," or some such title, we would all see at once how important it was. We could then take it into account, like Monsieur Jourdain discovering that what he had been speaking all his life was prose.

The reason there can be no miracles lies in this human capacity to take for granted. It would be miraculous if the sun stood still only because the sun does not stand still. Whatever happens is considered ordinary; a miracle is what does not happen. The sense of the miraculous is something else, an evanescent feeling of incredulity that seizes us at the first awareness of a change in nature, before there has been time to take it for granted. Only that first quarter inch seems miraculous; the second day's growth arouses no wonder. I began by chronicling a miracle which, when it occurred, was no longer such. This spectacular transformation of the earth took place, it now seems, as a matter of course; it would have been miraculous if it had not taken place. So we reduce the universe to the scope of our appreciation.

Yet the sense of the miraculous may persist as an accompaniment in one's inner ear to the music of the seasons. Recalling the bleak days of January, I cannot quite take for granted this present. The feeling of incredulity remains and is repeatedly aroused. The appearance of that first yellow-throated warbler in late March—just so in his established conformation, his movements, and his song—did not seem to me a necessity of nature. Likewise now, I wonder at the various kinds of warblers that are beginning to swarm in the woods, each a microcosm, a distinct being with its unique traits and features. I cannot say to myself: of course the chestnut-sided warbler has a yellow crown,

and of course the parula warbler does not; of course the
Kentucky warbler sings this phrase and the redstart
this other; of course the ovenbird has this carriage and
bearing. On what basis were these determinations orig-
inally made, and why a parula warbler at all? Nature
appears so completely the artist here, and so prolific,
that I find it hard to believe in any blind physical necessity as the cause of so much loveliness in such variety.

———————

The redstart, *Setophaga ruticilla,* is no less a fact in
this world than man, *Homo sapiens.* It shares man's
descent from some fishlike creature, was perhaps as
long in the making, and for all I know has equal im-

portance in the ranks of nature. If there is a reason
for man there is undoubtedly a reason for the redstart.
If man was cast in the image of his Maker, I should
think that so was the redstart.

Possibly excepting the parula warbler, the redstart is
the commonest warbler resident in Washington for the

breeding season. It sings and flits among the twigs in every copse and patch of woodland. The male is chiefly black, licked with orange flame on wings, tail, and sides of breast. Few warblers are so easy to find in the woods and to observe, since it is generally unhidden, preferring bare twigs and branches to the cover of dense foliage. Its behavior and action are its principal charm. In the openwork fringes of the trees it is the most acrobatic of aerial dancers, appearing to have virtually no weight; like thistledown on the wing, or like a small butterfly performing its evolutions. By comparison, the hummingbird has the mass of a bullet. Yet the redstart is adroit and quick. It has a way of tumbling down through a tree, from twig to twig to branch, fluttering and falling and darting, as nimble as quicksilver, as sure as a ball in a slot, spreading its black-and-orange tail like a blazon to the sunlight.

The song of the redstart is a brief series of high-pitched squeaky notes, often with an emphatic flourish at the end. It is variable in rhythm and emphasis, but not in its characteristic squeakiness. The little bird pauses every few moments in its dartings and flutterings to utter it, vibrating bill tilted slightly upward, tail shaking with the wholehearted effort. All this is the behavior proper to the redstart, let other birds behave as they may.

The redstart appears to have no fear of man and no interest in him. You will see one dart and flutter and drop from the trees to bathe in a leafy pool of rain water at your feet, as if you were invisible. Once I climbed to within reach of a redstart's nest high in a tree on the slope above Rock Creek. Though my hand was only inches from the nest, the flaming little male came repeatedly to feed the young as if he did not see me there.

The Kentucky warbler is as common as it can be during the breeding season in Washington, for I think that every square foot of its habitat belongs to the territory of one pair or another. It cannot be as common as the redstart if only because each pair requires a larger territory for its breeding, as it seems to me, from which all others of the species must be excluded. You hear the Kentucky warblers continually in the woods about the city, wherever there is good ground cover, but see them uncommonly. They are among the most difficult of warblers to observe, although they remain on the ground or low in the woods, and are bold of manner and conspicuous in color and markings. They are olive-green above, yellow below, with black on the forehead and face extending boldly down each side of the throat like mustaches. The eye has a yellow ring against the black to set it off. Like many birds that feed on the ground in the woods it has a short tail. It is awkward business on rough ground, as grackles and thrashers might testify, to have a long train always threatening to drag. Length of leg is another common feature of birds that spend much of their time on the ground in the woods. The Kentucky warbler, if it does not actually have longer legs than the more arboreal warblers, at least gives that impression by standing high on them. It comes to the same thing. When you do get a glimpse of the bird, it is generally displaying an excited alertness in every line of its body. It often appears to be straining upward with alertness in all its members, not only standing high on its legs, but head and tail pulled upward as if by threads, and even the little feathers on the top of its head raised in a sort of startlement.

Most little birds of the woods, when you follow them, move away from you a few feet at a time, flitting from one tree or bush to the next. The Kentucky warbler is hard to observe simply because it makes off completely on its first streaking flight, leaving you to explore the woods in an effort to find it all over again, when again it makes off. The only advantage this offers to the observer of its ways is that it enables him to determine easily the boundaries of a breeding bird's territory, for I think it tends to fly, when pursued, completely across its territory from one boundary to the opposite, and it is so persistent a singer that you always know by ear where it is. After you have put it up a few times, you find that it has demarcated the limits of its demesne for you. But you can waste hours of effort without getting more than an occasional half-glimpse of the bird itself, though its song rings repeatedly through the woods. You are as likely to see it by accident as by design.

The Kentucky warbler throws his head way back to sing. The song may be set down thus: the syllables *t'lee-t'lee-t'lee-t'lee-t'lee* uttered rapidly, in ringing tones, but in the perfunctory manner of most warblers. That remarkable singer, the Carolina wren, which lives alongside the Kentucky warbler, has the same syllables in its repertory, but utters them with a fullness or contralto huskiness of tone. The Kentucky warbler calls *chip* repeatedly, when it is excited, with a loudness and quality that enables you to recognize it in spite of all the other birds that also say *chip*.

The hooded warbler also is at home in the lower growth of deep woods, but appears to prefer relatively dry upland to the wet woods of the Kentucky warbler. Not feeding on the ground, it has a longer tail, a more vertical bearing, and less conspicuous legs than the Kentucky warbler. It, too, is green above and yellow below, but it wears black on its head like a fantastic hood with a large opening for the yellow face to show through. It also throws its head back on its shoulders, bill pointing skyward, to sing. Its song is delivered *con brio,* the most energetic of warbler songs, I think, not excepting that of the ovenbird: rapid, loud, unequivocal, and absolutely decisive in its punctuation and final flourish. It ends with a period, having delivered its message.

The worm-eating warbler is an unspectacular bird of wooded slopes for which, from year to year, I have felt an increasing appreciation. Neither its appearance, its manners, nor its song invites the vulgar attention. It is a little green bird with black stripes on its head, not common anywhere, quiet and less nervous of manner than most warblers. You hardly know what a good thing you have when you first discover it. The song is generally described as being almost indistinguishable from the fine trill of the chipping sparrow, but I find it easily distinguishable in that its quality is musical. The plain bird in its plain way sits on the branch of a tree in the shady woods and delivers its plain song. At first the bill is tilted up only slightly, but it is raised higher and opened wider in its vibrations during the short period of the single phrase. The musical trill is all on one pitch, a sleepy song, like a long snoring inhalation. It gives the impression in its regular and easy delivery that it is as automatic as breathing, which I think it is. It is like a part of the forest breathing gently.

I never saw a gull you would not take for a gull or a duck that seemed anything else than a duck, but you would probably not regard the Louisiana waterthrush, the northern water-thrush, and the ovenbird as warblers if you did not have the word of science for it. The evolution of the water-thrushes apparently had that of the spotted sandpiper as its model. They hold themselves horizontally and walk about like the sandpiper. They are streaked underneath as it is spotted, and like it have a light stripe over the eye. They share a habitat with the sandpiper in the wooded shores of streams, where like miniature sandpipers they run about on mudbanks and over rocks, poking their bills at insects. Strangest of all, they have the sandpiper's eccentric habit of teetering—that is

to say, of continually hoisting the rear end above the level of the rest of the body, in a sort of seesaw fashion. This must be useful in attracting insect prey. I have seen in both the sandpiper and the water-thrushes how, when they are hunting in shadow along the bank of a stream, the repeated momentary revelation of the white undertail coverts is like the flashing of a light. When the mockingbird is hunting insects on the ground, it repeatedly spreads its wings and tail to show the white in them, for what I guess to be the same reason.

The song of the Louisiana water-thrush is undoubtedly designed to be heard above the roar of tumbling water, for it is loud and piercing, three sharp notes followed by a chatter: *tzee-tzee-tzee-tzippy-tzippytzip*. It is given from the ground or from the branch of a tree, the singer throwing its head back.

Farther north you hear the ovenbird in season from every patch of woodland. In and about Washington you hear it from every other patch. It is generally a strident, disembodied voice, thought to repeat the word *teacher* (*chertea* would be more accurate) in ever-increasing volume to a pitch of apparent exasperation, at which it stops. The birds of Washington are distinct from those farther north, however, in that they tend to say *teach* instead of *teacher*. Having discovered this, I can tell the transient ovenbirds from our residents in the spring. The one-syllable birds arrive first and, of course, stay on after the others have gone north.

The ovenbird is a little streaked groundwalker in the deep woods. It carries itself like a miniature hen, its body horizontal, its breast rounded, its head high, and its short tail cocked straight up over its back. So it walks about with henlike dignity among the dead leaves and twigs, looking for something to peck at. It also mounts to low branches and walks along them. It is a sober bird of the dark woods, an inspector of their nethermost parts and foundations, climbing over twigs and debris, pausing to report itself regularly in the course of its rounds. You hear it commonly and see it rarely.

The black-and-white warbler, striped like a zebra, is an inspector of trunks and branches in the big timber. It fits against the bark. It is as properly placed and at ease underneath as atop a horizontal limb. There is no right side up. It can sing from any position, when the moment comes, its thin, high *zeewee-zeeweezeeweezeeweezeewee*. It can also whirl about on the

wing like a redstart to a new landing, and like the
redstart it appears to be fearless of man.

———————

All these are warblers that stay to nest in the big
woods of the city. Chats and Maryland yellowthroats
have their summer residence in the low and brushy
second growth, the prairie warblers at the edge of
open fields, and the yellow warblers wherever trees
stand apart from one another in the open. Spring
brings in addition the hosts of transient warblers,
some common and others rare, that pass through on
their way to nesting grounds farther north. The blackpoll warblers are the most abundant of these and, although the first to arrive in early May, they are the
last to depart. During the month of their passage you
can hear all day in the woods and parks, until you
come to identify it with the silence and so hardly hear
it any more, the little string of notes, high and thin,
all on one pitch, that is their song. They come sifting
through the treetops on their way north, inspecting
every leaf. At the peak of their abundance you do not
have to search for them; you need hardly do more
than look up to see them moving along in the treetops, periodically uttering their modest succession of
notes. The relatively big myrtle warblers, boldly
marked and easily identified by their flashes of yellow, are almost as common in April. The blue-and-
yellow Canada warblers, identifying themselves even
when unseen by the energetic chatter of their song,
are common for about ten days in the middle of May.
Chestnut-sided warblers, golden-winged warblers, and
black-throated-green warblers are somewhat less common, as are the black-throated-blue warblers drawl-
ing their slow songs in the deep woods. Both the
black-throated-blue and the black-throated-green sing

like musical insects, buzzing sleepily. You will find an occasional little Wilson's warbler, yellow with a black cap on the very crown of the head only, chattering in the underbrush for a few days in mid-May or later; a few blue-winged warblers, perhaps two or three of the bright and spectacular magnolia warblers, probably one or two Blackburnian warblers with flaming throats, a couple of Nashville warblers or a Tennessee warbler, and then if luck is with you a Cape May or a bay-breasted warbler. The game is to go out amid this abundance and variety to test your skill at discovery. But the game is only an excuse for enjoying the large munificence, which is the real discovery.

These warblers have progressed to their perfection ahead of us men. They are completely formed, they have realized themselves; we are still blundering along the way to a like realization of ourselves. The redstart is beyond striving to be anything different from itself and knows just what being itself calls for. It does not envy the wood thrush its size or seek to imitate its song. It does all that it is proper for a redstart to do, and only that. In every circumstance that confronts it, it reacts without hesitation and without thought after the fashion of its kind. It is itself—completed, perfected, accepted. The ideal redstart has its full manifestation in any redstart. The actuality is perfect. This is one reason why the redstart must be an object of admiration to men who, if asked to be themselves, would have to answer that they must first complete the evolutionary process of determining their own identity. Where shall we find a flesh-and-blood embodiment of ideal man? Let him stand forth who has achieved that perfection, whose form is the essential human form, his carriage the human carriage; who knows what it is proper for man to do in every circumstance; who is without uncertainty or room for improvement. "If men were as much men as lizards are lizards," said D. H. Lawrence, "they would be more worth looking at."

The honeybee is descended, I take it, from the same bit of protoplasmic slime as man. For a long period in the course of its evolution, the independent individual bee, in itself, must have been the central fact and representation of beedom. The individual must have existed, as such, before the society. The instinctive bee behavior that is now so automatic and inescapable was not always so. Perhaps there was intelligence at one stage. The individual discovered certain advantages in association, such as the economical division of labor, which made for a higher standard of living. The bee associations must have begun by being relatively free, voluntary associations, based on a free perception of what appeared best. These associations, as they became more complex and as the individuals within them grew more interdependent, gave rise to increasingly grave social problems. It was all very well, in the early stages, to rely on the intelligence and moral discipline of the individual bee who knew how to make a socially responsible use of his freedom. Some simple rules and sanctions would suffice to protect the mass of bees against the irresponsible few. But as the social organization grew more complex, the division of labor more thorough, and the interdependence more complete, the exercise of freedom by the individual became an increasing threat to the security of the whole. The social machinery was finally so delicate and intricate that one or a few individuals could upset it, bringing chaos, suffering, and death to the many. Perhaps a strike by a few worker bees would paralyze the whole economy of the hive, threatening all its members with starvation. Obviously, the free exercise of individual intelligence, which had been the glory and the hope of beedom and had characterized its nearest approach to the godhead, and which had been initially responsible for the wonderful social organization, must be done away with. Bees must become slaves to the state so that the economic benefits of their association might be preserved.

The ancestral bees who had had the intelligence and foresight to develop these social relations, which at one period made beedom the increasing wonder of creation and brought out the finest qualities of the individual bee, had yet not had foresight enough to foresee that the development they were inaugurating might keep going of its own nature and might go too far, reducing bees at last to dumb slavery, blindness, and impotence. But that is what happened. It was left for other species, such as man, which had not yet embarked on the adventure, to attempt a realization of the ideal that beedom had missed. The age of the bees was over, they had completed their evolution; the age of man was yet to come.

As I look at human society today, which by its ingenuity has developed such resources that the throwing of a switch in a powerhouse can leave millions destitute, that the mere threat can reduce millions to slavery, I hope the powers that be have shown such indulgence to the experiment of life as still to hold some protoplasmic slime in reserve.

There was a man who dwelt by himself in the barren desert. He had always dwelt by himself in the desert and he had never thought about anything. There had never been anything to think about. Then, one day, there was something to think about. A swallow came out of the south, the first living creature he had ever seen. It came from the horizon, flying not far above the ground in the flowing and undulating manner of swallows. When it came to the man it opened its forked tail and veered off its course, returning again and again to flutter about him.

Now the man was a practical man; his bent was scientific. Confronted by the unknown, he did not ask himself, "What is the reason for this?" He asked, "How does this work and what is its use?" He reached out his hand and caught the fluttering bird, pulled at its wings with his fingers, broke it apart, examined it, and finally ate it. Thereupon he felt an immediate satisfaction of the appetite, and later a dissatisfaction at having no more bird to eat.

There was another man in the desert who had the same experience. The swallow came out of the south, flowing and undulating over the desert, checked itself with outspread tail when it came to the man, and fluttered about him. The man had never seen anything like this living being, with its fluttering wings, iridescent plumage, and forked tail. Confronted by the unknown, he asked himself, "What is the reason for this?"—or, more simply, "Why?" This was the first food for thought, for reasoning, he had ever had.

The swallow continued on its course at last. The question remained with the man; and, I may as well say at once, it was never answered. It had started him thinking, however. "Why?" led directly to "Whence?" and "Whither?" In his thought he projected himself beyond the horizon that had hitherto bounded his world, projected himself in the direction from which the swallow had come and in the direction it had gone. He wondered about the source of life and about the end of life, which is to say that he embarked on the philosophical adventure. I shall not recount the steps of that adventure, since it is fully recorded in many volumes and since it certainly did not lead to the final answer that was its object. Its effect on the man is perhaps all that makes this story worth telling.

In the first place, it comforted him to know, by contemplation of the fact, that he was not the only living being, and in the enjoyment of this comfort he felt the emotion of love. He felt that the world contained good, and this good became the object of aspiration. Furthermore, he discovered the faculty of reason in the very asking of the first question, and how to apply this faculty to his aspiration. His reasoning led him to an appreciation of the Unknown; that is to say, it informed him that there was such a thing as the Unknown, that it existed. He was persuaded that the good had its origin in the Unknown, and this gave him his first personal bearings in a spacious world of reality. His own personality, which was capable of appreciating the good, must have a source in the same Unknown and, by reason of its aspiration, a destiny that gave it meaning. He began to value himself, not so much by what he was as by what he might become. Because he valued himself by something that was greater than he and beyond his ken, although he had the faculty to conceive of its existence, he also learned personal humility. Wonder, love, self-respect, and humility became the essential elements of his nature.

In telling the stories of these two men, I put the scientist before the philosopher; but in human history it is the other way around. The question that incessantly frames itself on the child's lips is "Why?" It would be easier for us adults if the child would ask "How?", for that is our own preoccupation. We have fallen into the habit of taking the world for granted as to its origins and meanings; so much so that the persistent curiosity of the child seems to us senseless if not downright perverse. "Just because!" we answer impatiently.

In our present-day preoccupation with scientific accomplishment, we are apt to overlook the fact that the great human cultures had their origin in philosophical rather than scientific enterprise. Classical culture, from its barbaric origin in Homeric days through its culmination in the days of Plato and Aristotle, was preoccupied with "Why?" Only later, during the materialistic period of its Roman decline, was it pre-eminently concerned with "How?" The Romans, practical people like ourselves, were more interested in making life work than in understanding it. Their successors were the benighted barbarians of the "Dark Ages" in Western Europe—for the Byzantine East had continued the Greek tradition and maintained its enlightenment.

The great civilized culture of modern times had its origin when, after a millennium of barbarism during which the shackles of Latinity worked loose, the child-like peoples of Western Europe began once more to ask "Why?" and turned to the ancient Greek philosophers for the answer. For the pursuit of "Why?" has an ennobling and uplifting effect on mankind, whereas "How?" administers to its appetites but fails to sustain its spirit. The essential sterility of science is evident in our own contemporary decline and fall.

"How?" not "Why?" is the question that concerns the slavish bee before the flower. The skill of the hive is science.

———————

To recapture the natural fresh wonder of the mind before the spectacle of life, imagine what must be the response of the intelligent anchorite, who has never known anything but lifeless desert, to the visitation of the swallow. The swallow is a supernatural being by reference to his own knowledge of nature. For the supernatural is merely what is strange to accepted experience; it is not more incomprehensible in itself than the natural. The distinction we make between the two is not intrinsic; it is simply the distinction between those spectacles for which our appreciation has been dulled by custom and those for which it has not.

The anchorite experiences awe at what the swallow represents. Of course, he does not know what it represents, but his intelligence informs him that it must have responsible antecedents and a reason for being. This is an awe-inspiring thought, since it is reasonable for him to believe that the antecedents of life have both mastery over it and a purpose. Away off there in the south, beyond his vision, is a power that makes him humble. This swallow is the messenger of eternity.

Another emotion that it would be natural for the anchorite to experience, at least as soon as he made sure there was no harm in the swallow, would be delight. This is the response of the child to the initial assumption that life is good, or has good in it. In making this assumption he is judging life by his own self, and therefore cannot be mistaken. The swallow is beautiful.

It is evident that this single experience of the swallow has opened untold possibilities to the man in the desert. Appreciating that nothing can be more marvelous for reasonable belief. He will feel justified in aspiring to such an existence.

The anchorite represents a childlike view of life, comparable to that of the Homeric men and the men of the pristine Middle Ages, who expressed that view in the form of legend simply because abstracted truth does not lend itself to comprehension. You have to illustrate with swallow or saint. We are not today a childlike people. We are a jaded adult people who, in the course of constant exposure to the marvelous, have come to take it for granted—that strange faculty we have. There is, moreover, a sort of tacit understanding among us that we simply will not push our questions as far back as the Unknowable, that we will not subject ourselves to awe and humility. We will rather disregard the whole business. What we do appreciate is that we have physical appetites, and the service of a man's appetites can easily become his exclusive preoccupation. We do not know more today than the child or the philosopher; we have simply limited the area of our concern, and so we know less. This suffices to explain our cultural and moral decline.

Yet eternal nature remains all about us for our appreciation, when the time comes, and our redemption.

The northwest wind kept the atmosphere clear, not a cloud in the sky all day Sunday, April 22. It was so cold that, even at midday, in the sunshine, my fingers were stiff when it came to opening the lock on my bicycle. One drake (I had thought they were all gone) and thirteen female red-breasted mergansers put down on the lagoon opposite the Pentagon Building. A few green-winged teal remained at Four Mile Run. Greater and lesser yellowlegs were common. At Sheridan Point, on the way to Mount Vernon, the first kingbird of the year flew across the highway and landed on top of a roadside tree. It was quite silent, which is not the kingbird's custom. Over the river were mixed swarms of swallows, including tree, barn, bank, and rough-winged swallows. That eccentric hermit of the brush, the white-eyed vireo, first of the year, was singing *stick-suwee-fiddle-stick* from the interior of a bush near Mount Vernon. Other new arrivals were red-eyed vireos, prairie warblers, Maryland yellowthroats, and redstarts.

The marsh vegetation at Dyke had now reached maturity. Rosebushes were in bloom along the highway, but the dogwood had only remnants of blossom.

The morning of April 25 was overcast; a heavy dripping mist in the woods as an aftermath of the preceding day's interminable drizzle and rain. It continued to rain fitfully, hard and soft, until late afternoon, when a new wind from the west cleared the sky of all but fleece remnants and the sun shone.

In the morning one drake scaup was preening his breast on a mound of earth in the excavation of East Potomac Park, disregarding the dump truck and workmen nearby, as the workmen disregarded him.

Dawn the next morning was windless. Sunshine on haze made a rainbow over the river. The first scarlet tanager was heard, in the park on my way to work.

I received a clue today to a question that had puzzled

me. Every spring you find bobwhites about the woods of Massachusetts Park, and always a pair at the edge of the woods where the veeries nested. You hear their vibrant calls, like human whistles at a distance, you sometimes see them marching by in the grassy undergrowth, and on occasion I have seen a hen leading her school of chicks across the street. Since the bobwhites belong to a group of birds that are not migratory, their short wings being inadequate for long flights, the question is what becomes of them in winter, when there is never a sign of them.

This evening, as Og and I were bicycling along the river just above Constitution Avenue, two bobwhites came hurtling across the river as though they had been catapulted from the opposite bank and, with whirring wings, fell into some bushes near the statue of William Jennings Bryan. Apparently the bobwhites are, after all, to some extent migratory. They would not casually undertake such a flight, which must be on its scale the counterpart of what the flight across the Gulf of Mexico is to the barn swallows.

No bird is more heartwarming to watch than the bobwhite, in the diffidence and simplicity of its behavior, as well as in its plump appearance. It is like a child in a world of ogres. When it runs, instead of leaning forward in the manner of robins and all orthodox runners, it stretches itself up as high as it can, making itself tall, its feet working so quickly and smoothly beneath it that it seems to be on wheels.

I never see that black seafowl, the cormorant, except when I least expect it. The cormorant is endowed with a train of literary associations that has made its name synonymous with rapacious greed. The gloating prophet Isaiah threatened mankind with it, "for the indignation of the Lord is upon all nations." Aristotle described its habits. Sir Thomas More attacked the practice of sheep culture, which was replacing tillage, as "that one covetous and unsatiable cormorant . . ." The king in *Love's Labour's Lost* refers to "cormorant devouring Time." Old John of Gaunt, in *Richard the Second*, speaks of "light vanity, insatiate cormorant" in his denunciation of the king's greed. One of the Roman citizens in *Coriolanus*, after having listed "the counsellor heart, the arm our soldier, our steed the leg, the tongue our trumpeter," adds "the cormorant belly." In *Troilus and Cressida* the terms offered by Nestor to Priam are:

Deliver Helen, and all damage else,
As honour, loss of time, travail, expense,
Wounds, friends, and what else dear that is consum'd
In hot digestion of this cormorant war,
Shall be struck off.

John Caius wrote in 1570 that the cormorant "Is endowed by nature with only one intestine straight and without a coil . . . on account of the vehemence of the natural heat, which very quickly consumes all that it swallows."

The word "cormorant" itself was produced by the wearing and polishing action of many tongues through many ages on the original Latin words, *corvus marinus*, meaning sea raven—and with "raven" we associate "ravenous." The cormorant is the ravenous creature of the sea. It pursues fish fathoms below the surface, and catches them. Its gullet stretches to accommodate prey wider than itself. In China, tame cormorants, with rings on their necks to prevent swallowing, are used for fishing. Cormorants are represented in paintings of the Ming Dynasty by Lin Liang and Pa Ta Hsien. E. H. Forbush cites Dr. Charles W. Townsend as reporting that, after a certain trading schooner had sunk off the Labrador coast, the cormorants on a nearby island decorated their nests with pocketknives, pipes, hairpins, and ladies' combs that they salvaged from the bottom of the sea.

The sun rose brilliantly in a clear sky the morning of May 4. As it rose, however, milky clouds steamed up all about the horizon, as if the process of the sun "burning off" the mist had been reversed. Against this setting, a glossy black cormorant with snaky neck stretched forth, like a hybrid fowl between raven and goose, was flapping in circles over the river near the Highway Bridge.

The evening of May 10 another cormorant flew north, flapping low over the housetops along Connect-

icut Avenue. Over Dupont Circle it flew, beating against the wind; over Small's, the Florist; over Copenhaver's stationery store and Walpole's linen shop; over Pierre's Restaurant—and on to the Gulf of St. Lawrence, for all I know. In Whyte's Bookshop & Gallery, across the avenue, no one knew that a figure of ancient literature had just passed.

Georgetown, now incorporated into the city of Washington, is where the West begins. It is a frontier town at the edge of the cultivated piedmont, the last seaport, a gateway to the Ohio Valley, the Mississippi basin, the illimitable French and Indian wilderness of the interior. Georgetown is where the men of the eighteenth century, if they ventured farther at all, changed into buckskin. Thus far they sailed from Europe on the pleasant tidewater reaches of the Potomac, past formal country estates and plantations; beyond, they mounted the shaggy slopes of the Appalachian chain, across the Blue Ridge and the mountain valley of the Shenandoah or through Cumberland Gap, into the interior of a continent.

Above Georgetown the Potomac River flows in rapids, through gorges, and about wooded islands. The construction of a navigable canal up the river into the interior was initially undertaken by General George Washington. The Chesapeake & Ohio Canal, designed to connect with the Ohio River at Pittsburgh, was completed as far as Cumberland by the middle of the nineteenth century, when the development of railways made further construction uneconomical. It remained in service, however, as one of the routes of trade with the interior of North America, until the twentieth century, being finally abandoned as such in 1924. The frogs and water plants inherited man's handiwork. Then, in 1938, the federal government was inspired to purchase the canal in its entire length and restore it, as an historic monument, for twenty-two miles above Georgetown, to Seneca Feeder Locks.

At its lower end, where it empties into Rock Creek, the Chesapeake & Ohio Canal lacks majesty. It is an obscure littered ditch running under the streets and between the brick walls of Georgetown; a place to throw a corpse. On the other side of town, it is an avenue of water between high banks supporting shade trees and shrubbery. The towpath, along the side nearer the river, provides a promenade for Sunday citizens. The atmosphere is pastoral. Little boys fish, not with flies for art's sake, but with worms for the unaccomplished pleasure of it. Throwing stones at frogs is another sport. The wild wilderness begins farther along.

We generally take to the towpath some twenty miles upriver, at Pennyfield Locks, and well before dawn. The dirt road winds steeply down from the rolling hills of Maryland and comes to an end on the inner bank of the canal. There is a farm and country house here. The little lockhouse is of whitewashed stone on the other side, glimmering in the dark. You can cross the canal to it by walking on the slanting wooden arms of the locks by which you swing them open and shut. This is generally done in late starlight. Then turn right, being very quiet, talking only briefly and in hushed voices, and walk up the towpath a couple of hundred yards. The birds have begun to sing, though it is still night. Whippoorwills are calling steadily in the distance. A barred owl hoots four times—*who cooks for you?*—and again—*who cooks for yooooou-all?* The cardinals are singing, each note slipping its pitch. That is a wood thrush on the other side of the canal now, and robins steady in the distance. An Acadian flycatcher overhead repeats a single note from

moment to moment; then the faint musical trill of its wings as it flutters them, decelerating at the end.

From directly across the canal, two good frog leaps away in the darkness, comes a single loud musical note like a plucked string; then another; then a caw; then a row of notes, all on one pitch, starting in quick succession and becoming slower until they stop altogether; then another caw and the sound of laughter. This is the humorous chat. A redstart is singing its squeaky song. Wood thrushes are caroling here, there, elsewhere. . . .

The trees stand out as silhouettes against a pale sky from which the stars are vanishing. A breeze comes ruffling among the leaves and caresses the backs of our necks. What was first a casual tuning up of bird voices has become a steady and clamorous chorus. It requires mental concentration to pick out the single voice and identify it. You have to shut your mind, for the moment, to all other voices, or divide it into parts. It is a case of listening with all one's ears. (When we were in school we played a game that provided training for this art. Two of us would read aloud simultaneously from different books while the third listened and, at the end, was required to give a circumstantial account of what had been read from each book. If that was too easy, three books were read simultaneously. So far only was it practicable for us to go. But here the voices are innumerable and, if we are to listen intelligently, we must be constantly selecting from among them, excluding the multitude for the moment of concentration.) "What is that?" says one of us, listening perhaps to one lisp in the hundredfold chorus, and since we cannot tell what he hears we must answer: It is all creation singing!

By this time you can say it is daylight. The stars are gone and we look about for the first time. Behind, as we face the canal, is a thin line of big timber and shrubbery, then a marsh, then another line of trees at the edge of the river. Across the canal is a wilderness of swampy woods, an inaccessible great forest holding black water between its roots, where strange beasts might remain unknown. In the gray light of dawn a pair of wood ducks, crying loudly, come hurtling out of this forest, set their wings, and splash down into the still canal. For a moment they rest in dim silhouette, silent, heads strained upward with alertness . . . then leap away again, crying again, and fly back into the woods farther up the canal.

We turn and start walking slowly up the towpath.

In the overhanging branches you hear the harsh *spee* of the blue-gray gnatcatchers. The tiny birds are fluttering and darting about like moths at the fringes of foliage, collecting cobweb from the nests of tent caterpillars to build their own nests. Scarlet tanagers, Kentucky warblers, Louisiana and northern water-thrushes, redstarts, parula warblers, wood thrushes, wood pewees, crested flycatchers, Acadian flycatchers, song sparrows, cardinals, goldfinches, purple finches, indigo buntings, red-bellied woodpeckers, flickers, downy woodpeckers, mourning doves, catbirds, red-eyed vireos, yellow-throated vireos, Maryland yellowthroats, crows, titmice, Carolina chickadees, blackpoll warblers, red-winged blackbirds, and cowbirds are all singing or calling together. These are the constant sounds in the chorus. A yellow-billed cuckoo across the canal emits a rapid series of *cuks* and *cows*. Farther up the canal a black-billed cuckoo limits itself to an irregular series of *cuks* at intervals. Most grateful to our ears, almost lost in the chorus, is the soft, aspiring music of an olive-backed thrush singing repeatedly from the woods opposite. We have already heard a black-throated-green warbler, two Canada warblers, and a golden-winged warbler.

A towpath by a canal in the first half of May has everything to recommend it. Being flat, smooth, and relatively straight, you move along it quietly without need to watch your step; you can keep your eyes on trees and bushes. The canal makes a broad opening through the woods, a long vista in which your vision has scope. Birds are always most abundant where there is water, as here. If this canal had been designed for the observation of birds rather than for commerce with the West it could not have been better done.

We have come to the end of the marsh on our left. Between the canal and the river now is a depressed alluvial flat supporting trees whose immense trunks rise at pitched angles from the soft ground, chiefly sycamores, silver maples, and big river birches. They have sunk over sideways. There is not much underbrush; you can walk freely about the great boles if you wish. The density is all overhead, where the leaning trees branch and branch again until they are all interlaced and screen the sky. Across the canal the ground rises firmly and steeply, a forest of oaks, tulip trees, and beeches, with thick undergrowth. The canal is dark here, for the dense heads of the trees reaching across it make a canopy; it runs through a lacework tunnel. Here you pause to listen to the varied and constant chorus of birds, unequaled elsewhere. . . .

A female wood duck swimming rapidly away up the dappled canal is followed by nine little balls of black scurrying over the water to keep up with her. She makes for the steep bank and climbs into the marginal grass, the ducklings scrambling after and disappearing. Then she splashes back into the water alone and proceeds to thrash about, rowing herself away from the bank with splashing wings to distract us from her hidden young. After a minute of this she flies up and off. In the steep woods across the canal a worm-eating warbler is repeating regularly its long musical inhalation. A black-throated-blue warbler is singing. A sudden yelping comes from back in these woods, starting, leaving off, starting again: one of the big pileated woodpeckers, which so rarely show themselves, is calling.

On the alluvial flat below the towpath the trunk of a silver maple leans toward the river. Fifteen feet above-ground, a large hole leads to some inner darkness. Our curiosity aroused by a bit of down stuck to its lower rim, I take up a dead limb from the ground and hurl it crashing against the trunk. Instantly a wood duck appears in the opening, hoists herself through in one movement, and flies away.

The canal curves to the right here and its setting changes abruptly. Only the towpath and a line of shrubbery intervene between it and the river below, which flows in boisterous roaring cataracts past rocks and brush-covered islands. Spotted sandpipers run about on the rocks and get their feet wet. Here, like as not, you see an osprey or an eagle sweeping over the river. Kingbirds rise steeply on fluttering wings from the islands, capture their insect prey, and glide back to perch with tails spread. Across the canal is a jutting cliff, its face roughly broken with hollows and shallow ledges, twisted cedars perched high above. A pair of phoebes nest every year in a cranny, barons of the cliff, protected by high walls and a moat, enjoying a splendid view of the world below.

The sun is up now and its first rays, springing across the landscape, charge the atmosphere with radiant heat. This is the ultimate luxury. No one can properly appreciate sunlight, I think, who does not go out before dawn.

At one point, where big trees again rise above the towpath, lighted directly by the sun, one is bound to find the rarest of local birds, the cerulean warbler. It is always here in May, revealing its presence by its quick buzzing song, incessantly repeated from the treetops. The cerulean warbler is a bird of the Middle West, belonging properly on the other side of the Appalachian boundary, but it has apparently spilled over the mountains at Cumberland and trickled down the Potomac Valley. It is here, every year in the same place, and there are records for eastern Maryland. Because it is such a rarity, and because it is hard to see in the tops of the tall trees, we always take time to hunt it out, to obtain at least one glimpse of the quick blue-and-white bird with the black line across its breast.

The feeder locks, below Seneca, mark the end of the restored section of the canal. Here a low embankment

has been built out into the river, which is again broad
and placid above it, though tumultuous below, and
from its abutment a short feeder canal connects with
the main canal by way of the locks. Below this embankment the river sings and gushes through a network of
channels among islands covered with water-resistant
brush and low trees. Here is the home of that shining
wonder among birds, the prothonotary warbler. I suppose the members of the College of Prothonotaries
Apostolic, in the Roman Church, wear blue and gold

vestments. This is a bright golden warbler with dark eyes, blue wings, and blue tail. It perches on open twigs and branches overhanging water and throws its head back to utter its loud, plain *tweet, tweet, tweet, tweet.* Then it darts across the water to another perch and sings again. Its golden, almost orange body plumage has a deep velvety quality, like that of the scarlet tanager, which gives it a loveliness of texture beyond its loveliness of color when seen in direct sunlight. There is a pair or, perhaps, a small colony of prothonotary warblers at Dyke, and a small colony here. It is a rare warbler. I have watched a pair here in their courtship, the male bowing and dancing along a limb in sunlight, opening his tail like a fan to show

the white at the corners, before finally mounting the crouching and fluttering female. Then off they go like darts and you hear the song again, above the roar of water, from some islet farther down.

Beyond the feeder locks the canal is unrestored, an empty moat clogged with saplings. Catbirds, chats, and white-eyed vireos are vociferous in the undergrowth, indigo buntings sing their constant and monotonous songs. Where Seneca Creek (a little river in itself, flow-

ing straight through a tunnel of big trees) empties at
right angles into the Potomac, a summer bungalow
colony has grown up as naturally as a colony of bees in
a hollow tree. There are abandoned locks and a lock-

house here, and the canal, with its towpath, crosses the
creek on a triple-arched stone bridge. The scene from
the bridge presents a varied and pleasant view, looking
down on the world. It embraces the colony of men moving about their affairs along both banks of the creek,
beneath the overarching trees; and a community of
swallows, barn and rough-winged. The swallows swarm
in and out under the heavy stone arches, swerving below and shooting past with such deft celerity that the
eye cannot follow. One could sit here happily all day,
feet hanging over, watching life.

A long stone's throw above Seneca Creek is a marsh
hidden from the path by a border of catbird cover. It
is really a shallow lake camouflaged by marsh grass, cat-
tails, and clumps of willow. This is the last point of
special interest on the excursion. In early or mid-May
you will generally find one or two pairs of ducks feeding here, probably blue-winged teal, perhaps baldpates,
on one occasion ringnecks. As you wade out into the
marsh, squishing with your feet, they swim behind

clumps of grass or willow, heads high, trying to persuade themselves that you cannot see them. They are always reluctant to leave this feeding ground. Indeed, the teal, when your approach finally impels flight, are likely to circle away and return, putting down again in the channels between hummocks, behind willows. If you make no disturbance and do not stare too rudely at them (this last is important in observing any bird), they finally relax their attention and resume tipping up to feed. This is also the place to look for solitary sandpipers and, perhaps, a company of least sandpipers so unsuspicious that they walk about and feed fearlessly almost at your feet.

It must have been noted by others that nothing in nature is vulgar, in the common use of that term. Vulgarity, in all its varieties, is an attribute of civilized man, an offense not so much against conventional as against natural propriety. It is an expression of revulsion against propriety, against a too-delicate sense of propriety in others and in oneself, against the tyranny of "good taste." It is designed to blunt the edge of such sensitivity. Therefore it is an expression of man's spiritual restlessness, uncertainty, and dissatisfaction. If a redstart revolted against its own instinctive behavior, which represents a binding propriety, it might be vulgar and make a virtue of vulgarity; but it is always itself, not a half-creation like man but a completely realized ideal, a finished product.

I never have this feeling and this admiration more strongly than when I see the solitary sandpiper. It passes through Washington in late April and May on its way from South America and the Indies to its breeding grounds in Canada. Unlike others of its kind, which haunt beaches and open mud flats, it is a bird of woodland pools and streams. It prefers the perforated dome of foliage overhead and the mottled shade below, where you hear the sound of running water or the buzz of insects over still water. In Rock Creek you see it, most delicate of birds, standing at the edge of a gravelly bank in midstream, like a dark leaf on slender stalks. It takes off, springing from the bank, and flicks out over the water, showing its short white tail barred with black. Its wings are slender, pointed, darkening from gray to black at the tips. They cut deep, in one flick after another, quite unlike the rapid mechanical vibration of the spotted sandpiper. It does not ordinarily fly, under these circumstances, in a straight line, but wavers like a butterfly, appearing uncertain where to put down again. Legs hanging, it seems about to alight on a rock in midstream . . . when it veers off, and so wavers from one possible landing to another, almost touching and snapping away again, until at last its feet touch and it stands. I have seen it at its loveliest in this butterfly behavior on the canal where the water was shallow and showed banks of silt. Occasionally it will make off completely, however, and then it rises swiftly with no uncertainty and speeds away at the level of the treetops or crossing over them, crying *peet-weet*.

The combination of delicacy and robustness in nature, which the Chinese landscape painters made their theme, is one of the attractions of trees. It is what they might be considered as preaching to men, a sort of chivalric code applicable to all the ways of life. The masculine and feminine are not by nature at odds but in harmonious conjunction as parts of one whole.

As the robin is better known than the redstart, because more conspicuous, so the white and paper birches are better known and appreciated than the red or river birch. The two white-barked birches are not native so far south as this; the river birch, though it creeps up into the north, is a southern birch. It grows commonly wherever there is water to reflect it. Along the banks of Rock Creek, as at the edge of the canal, the round shafts of the trunks, covered in shaggy brown bark, generally spring from the ground at an angle, as if attracted toward the water, without any perceptible swelling or buttressing where they leave the ground. When they reach the point of branching, they do it handsomely, ordinarily dividing at first into two stout branches that spread apart in their ascent as if to embrace all space between them. The heads are open, the foliage a floating lacework of small leaves, showing the sky above in innumerable points of light. This river birch combines delicacy with a shaggy grandeur that is not ordinarily associated, at least in such degree, with its kind.

One of these days I shall select a prominent grove and place near it a signpost with an arrow and the message: "This Way to the River Birches." That will establish it among the sights of Washington. I confess that I had been looking for birds in the branches of this tree for years before I discovered the tree itself; and I have before me a book on the *Trees of Washington* that omits mention of it while stating in a tone of regret that birches prefer a more northerly climate. The native faculty of observation—at least in adult, civilized man— is largely a faculty for exclusion. Opening our minds to what our eyes behold is a cultivated art, a discipline acquired in response to curiosity. It has the immeasurable advantage, however, that no door of the mind thus opened is ever again shut. The understanding that results from it is cumulative and perpetual.

The silver maple is one of the common trees of Washington. It is a rugged tree in its full growth, branching low and spreading generously, though in a disorderly fashion. The bark is shaggy and silver-gray, but this is not what gives it its name. The deeply cut leaves are pale, almost white underneath, in contrast to the rich green of their upper surfaces. When the wind blows, the under surfaces are turned up and the exposed parts of the tree change from green to what appears as silver, momentarily covering the tree in gusts and evanescing like breath on a windowpane. When a gusty wind blows you can recognize the silver maples at the edge of the woods half a mile away by their shimmering bloom. They glint and brighten fitfully against a black storm-sky as the wind stirs them.

As the silver maple is seen at its silvery best on windy days, when it reveals its chief loveliness, so the two species of locust are at their best on still, sunny days. The comparatively slender stalks of the black locust often rise in clusters from the ground, in the woods or at the edge of the woods or bordering streets where they have been planted. The stalks have a wavering ascent, like seaweed, and the foliage is generally clustered in separate domes against them. Young trees, however, wear their foliage in tresses that cover them. The black locust at its best is delicate and unspectacular, improving with acquaintance. Its pinnate leaves, made up of leaflets balanced on a central shaft, clothe it as in a luminous green plumage that reveals its depth as the sunlight plays over it in subtle gradations. In the North a blight has afflicted the black locusts, which stand starkly in tragic silhouette of trunk and branch against the sky, bearing their surviving clusters of leaves like vine-wrapped ruins. Outside of Washington it is common to see dead branches on big roadside locusts, but in the city and in the woods they are generally in good foliage, especially those that have not attained mature age. It may be that they die gradually, limb by limb, persisting against the sky and still struggling to put forth young leaves as if they could escape mortality by refusing to acknowledge it.

Yet this locust in its youthful prime has a yielding delicacy and luxuriance of habit, like a girl reaching maturity without any experience of survival as a trial. In late April it puts forth a white inflorescense amid its green bowers, perfuming the passing breezes with a freshness and sweetness that must rejuvenate the very stones.

The honey locust gives an impression of greater sophistication. Its leaves are made up of finer and more numerous leaflets. I would not know how to distinguish them from small fern fronds if they did not grow aloft. They make fern patterns against the sky. The trunk is stouter, solider, altogether more robust than that of the black locust. The gray bark is hard, like armor plating or rhinoceros hide, and intricate clusters of thorns, radiating in every direction, grow out against the trunk and lower branches. The tree is thus openly on the defensive against terrestrial marauders. A thornless variety has been developed, however, that is more convenient for the city's innumerable squirrels.

(George Washington recorded in his diary that on Tuesday, March 21, 1786, he planted at Mount Vernon "between 17 and 18,000 seed of the honey locust.")

Both locusts, but especially the honey locust, have a distinct utility for the observer of migrating warblers. Most of these warblers, moving through the top of the woods, are effectively screened from below by the density of foliage. They come out into the open, however, where a locust or a grove of locusts holds the other trees back to let the sky show through. Here the observer may see them quite plainly above, flitting and dancing in the open tracery of twigs and branchlets and feathery fronds. No amount of patient artfulness under tulip tree or oak is worth the good sense of stationing oneself under a locust, just as the flycaster wastes his skill if he does not select the right pools.

If any one tree is dominant in the woods of Washington it is the tulip tree. The tulip tree is like an upright man: it has all the common virtues and no outstanding distinction—unless it be size. It tends to grow straight up, and is as tall and handsome as any tree. Its branches have a habit of angularity, changing their direction abruptly; but this shows chiefly in winter, when it stands bare, making its identification in this season possible at long distances. The leaves are big and square-cut. Toward the end of April large tulip-shaped green blossoms appear conspicuously all over the tree, providing a feast for the squirrels that leaves the ground beneath littered with its remains.

The beech is the classic sylvan tree. It is associated with parklike sloping glades in the deep woods, where it stands as a blue-barked aristocracy of its own. It is stout and firmly rooted in maturity, its trunk buttressed against the ground. In the woods where it grows to best advantage, and especially on dark, rainy days, its bark takes added color from the somberness of its surroundings, appearing bluer the more somber the light. Its leaves are a glossy dark green, but those that remain hanging to the tree in winter become white and sere. The beech has classical and literary associations that are inescapable. The aura of dryads is still about it. Its roots give refuge to elves. Pan knew it. It is surely the tree on which Orlando, in the Forest of Arden, carved the name of Rosalind. Robin Hood and his men were at home under the beeches of the New Forest. A sloping beech glade in the deep woods is hardly to be dissociated from thoughts of pastoral love and peacefulness. Here the doe nuzzles the spotted faun.

In the woods of Washington, as elsewhere, you will not find a mature beech on which the passing generations have not left the record of their passing. The tree has such an historic and enduring aspect, and its bark is so smooth, that it invites all those who seek to perpetuate the solitary moment to take out their pocket-knives and have at it. Simple initials and dates, carved on the stalwart trunks of beeches, are the only record left of moments of contentment or melancholy now ages past. A boy carves his initials on the beech with some assurance that, blurred but still decipherable, he may return to them as an old man and recapture in memory the emotion of a moment that had otherwise been lost.

In winter the columnar trunk and branches of a full-grown sycamore, mottled with flakes and patches of dark, generally show lighter than the sky behind, giving the tree a fairy aspect in spite of its immensity. On moonlight nights it stands in bony whiteness against the sky. The branches, ramifying into stiff twigs, are

like arms and fingers thrown out with vigorous aban-
don; they seem to have been struck motionless in mo-
tion. Few great trees have so much style. Its summer
leaves are large, silvery, and spaced apart to show
broad glimpses of skeleton.

The most impressive sycamores I have seen grow
about Washington—in the city and wild along the
banks of the Potomac. One of the largest in the city
stands with an aspect of ancient grandeur before the
refined marble façade of the Pan American Union. It
has a mute eloquence, like a Lear of the wilderness
transplanted to genteel surroundings.

In the second half of April the woods, in their fresh
foliage, exhibit to a distant view a motley and con-
trasting variety of green in shades ranging from near
yellow and silvery to the darkness of the beech leaves.
They are only less variegated in their initial luxuriance than in fall, when so many of the trees appear to
take fire, exhibiting their most brilliant colors in the
last gasp of the season like those fish that glow with
iridescent hues at the moment by death. By the middle of May the paler leaves have darkened and the
relative uniformity of the summer woods is established.

———————

Except in their periods of rest, birds generally mani-
fest such continuous alertness and vitality as a man
displays only in those rare moments when he exercises
his faculties to the utmost—when engaged in strenu-
ous athletic activity, or startled, or responding to
panic. The redstart, the robin, or the wood duck appears every moment alert in every faculty. A man
would be worn out in short order by such intensity
of living. This tautness and quickness of life in birds
is one of their principal attractions.

A pair of nighthawks comes each spring, arriving before the middle of May, to spend the summer in the residential and shopping area just north of Dupont Circle, where I suppose they nest on one of the flat roofs. In their own way they show that wonderful vitality, striding erratically across the sky on their long wings and calling. You see the male waving and snapping his wings at dusk, engaged in a sunset dance, facing into the wind, then letting it sweep him away, then coming about into it again. All the time his penetrating nasal *peent*, regularly repeated, punctuates the performance and calls attention to it. Then he dives from on high, plummeting below the housetops, to reappear a moment later, climbing and calling. You have the impression, watching him, that this display is an exhibition of natural virility in its essence.

———————

The tangled greenery of honeysuckle, where it grows in solid banks by the side of 28th Street and along Rock Creek Drive, showed the first incipient blossoms, peeping out among the leaves, on May 16. Within a week they were out in full abundance. Their perfume enticed the passer-by and worked so swooningly upon his brain that for the moment he knew the experience of the lotus-eaters. In late May there is a constant and pervasive freshness to the air of Washington, even in the crowded downtown streets, that I cannot explain except as the diffused effect of so much outlying honeysuckle in bloom.

———————

It is four-fifteen on the morning of May 21. The sleeping city is under assault. Bursts of cannonading resound in the night; lightning, wavering on and off, fitfully illuminates curtains of rain. The cannonading is heard above the steady roar of water cascading over the car in which we move through the streets. . . .

When we reached Dyke, at a quarter to five, the storm had passed. A dismal daylight was appearing as we made our way through pools of water, following the line of trees and shrubs along the spit that separates the marshes from the open bay. The tide was up, the marshes brimful. You could smell them: an odor of wetness and decay, aquatic animal life, steeped vegetation.

In full daylight now, though the sky remained overcast, we waded out knee-deep into the marshes, among the coarse grasses that rose above the level of our eyes, trying to walk on the wobbling hummocks. The trick of tramping in cold water is to get your feet as wet as possible right away, so that you no longer spoil your enjoyment by trying to keep dry. Away with that instinct! Let your boots fill with water at the start; it makes you free to go where you please.

This kind of wilderness, neither land nor plain water, is almost inaccessible to man. It remains virgin when armies and navies have passed. What the wide ocean is to the petrel, what the forest is to the woodpecker, this is to the long-billed marsh wren; but even more so, for while the petrel comes to land to nest, and woodpeckers are found in orchards, this wren is hardly imaginable in any other setting. Marsh grass is its cover and the support under its feet; it provides the material and the site for its nesting. The rest of the world is to the marsh wren what the ocean is to the warbler, a strange realm that it crosses on the wing at night in its migrations, no better than interstellar space.

We heard the wrens this morning before there was

light to see them. All over the marshes we heard them,
singing in a steady chorus, each song a gurgling chatter, brief but repeated with hardly time for breath
between. When it became light enough, we saw the
singing wrens as far as the eye could reach over the
marshes, carried upward on fluttering wings above the
grass-tops by the very exuberance of their song, and
sinking back again. The dots were bobbing up and
down everywhere, like a natural effervescence given
off by the marsh.

These wrens are among the smallest of birds, and
charged with an exuberant energy almost too great
for them to contain. They appear to be overwhelmed
and shaken by their own vitality. The response of any
individual, when we waded into his territory, was to
sing steadily, making his hidden way through the
reeds by short flits and jumps to within a few feet of
us, mounting occasionally into the open with one reed
in each foot to look at us and sing harder than ever,
but never staying still for more than a moment. Then
he would launch himself straight up above the reeds
to hover down again with legs hanging, singing all
the while. As evidence of his inner tension and excitement, moving from reed to reed, his little tail would
be cocked to the point where it almost touched the
back of his head. Some of the wrens were busy, even
while they watched us, collecting old dry strips of reed
and constructing their great nest-balls among the live
standing reeds; but they did not allow this activity
to interfere with singing.

The wrens were the principal feature, but the
whole marsh would have been alive even without
them. Kingbirds were engaging noisily in exhibitions
of power flight and aerial control. Redwings were crying and singing and flying wherever you looked. Twice
we alarmed a female wood duck in an inlet, each with

a flotilla of ducklings; the drakes were constantly rising and circling out over the marshes. Great blue herons trailed their legs in flight, an osprey was hunting, black ducks took off and put down here and there, quacking softly. Late as was the season, we surprised a lone female red-breasted merganser on an inlet and made her take the air, splashing over the still water to launch herself.

This was the day that I added the least bittern to

my circle of acquaintance. The first I flushed flew weakly over the grass-tops and dropped back into them beyond an inlet, where I could not follow. It was fantastic to me in the glimpse I had of it, not quite a duck by its small size, its flight, or its markings; nor a rail. I did not identify it until I flushed another in the same fashion later that day, this one a male, and recognized it by the bold black-and-cream markings on back and wings.

As music is the purest form of expression, so it seems to me that the singing of birds is the purest form for the expression of natural beauty and goodness in the larger sense, the least susceptible of explanation on ulterior practical grounds. The flight of the heron is as beautiful as the song of the thrush, but the heron flies as it does for other than aesthetic reasons. You might maintain that the color of the male scarlet tanager serves to intimidate his enemies and is only incidentally beautiful. It is harder to argue away the pure beauty of the thrush's song by considerations of utility. Whatever practical purpose it may be said to serve surely does not require such elaborate and studied loveliness. This is more than an incidental expression of beauty; it proclaims that the beautiful and good are elemental.

In the closing weeks of spring, after the principal wave of migration has passed and the birds are fewer, the center of interest is upon the late passage of the spotted thrushes. The best stage for these thrushes is the vicinity of the sylvan ravine where the veeries nested. Indeed, this cleft in the woods, with its natural moisture, its trees and the darkness beneath them, its undergrowth on the north slope and the open ground beneath the beeches across from it, with its tumbling brook and its precipitous rock formations, is a metropolis of birds. Entering it on a spring morning is like entering a cool cellar, except that there is a welcome freshness, a dewy pungency for the nostrils. It is like a thronged aviary in the abundance and variety of bird life. Most of the birds you see as movement rather than form, so quick they are and so deft about their business. You hear them around you, of course, and they come out in full view on the broad path, hopping about and hunting for insect fare in all the attitudes of alertness. The broken sunlight, falling slantwise in beams, streaks the haze between trees. One section of a beech tree will be radiant, every leaf illuminated. Elsewhere, coins of light are scattered across the gloom. The woods are half dark and half adazzle.

It is a common observation that neither veery, hermit thrush, nor gray-cheeked thrush sings on migration. This is not, I think, because they find singing incompatible with the process of migration. In the annual cycle of their existence the impulse to sing comes at a date when they have ordinarily completed migration. Therefore the exceptions to the rule of silence occur among the laggards; the song season begins on schedule, even though migration has not been completed.

At one time or another I have heard the full song of every one of the five spotted thrushes in my vale; and I have heard all but the hermit thrush sing there within the span of one hour. The hermit thrush I heard only once, on April 28, 1944. I was walking through the woods that sunny afternoon when suddenly, from down the ravine, came the shower of music in successive and mounting impulses, continuing for about ten seconds. Though it was not repeated, the memory of it has permanently enriched the scene.

The first migrating olive-backs arrive early in May, but it is toward the middle of May that you first hear their song, which is heard with increasing frequency

through the remainder of the month, until they become scarce and finally disappear during the first week
in June. In 1945 I saw my first olive-back in the vale
on May 9, and first heard the song there on May 11.

Most songbirds, especially those that have elaborate
or distinguished songs, are in full song only for a period preceding the activities of nesting and raising
young, and sometimes again for a briefer period after
the first brood has been raised. When they sing at
other times, the song is generally incomplete in its
phrasing though unreduced in volume. The olive-
back, like the veery and the mockingbird, reduces volume. It sings a whisper song, and you have to be close
by to hear it at all. But it is still the full song, the succession of musical bounds rising to the limit of audible
pitch and, undoubtedly, beyond. You can never quite
tell where the song leaves off. In its lower notes it has
a reedy quality that is more or less pronounced, depending on the particular singer or song. It might be
imitated on the oboe, if the oboe were capable of such
grace and could aspire so high. The quality of individual singers, of course, varies. The olive-back, when
alert, also utters a soft single note, as if a cello string
had been plucked and instantly muted.

The impression made by this song is often so mysterious that, in the spring of 1945, I was at pains to
attempt an occasional description of it in my daily
notes. I offer these here because they were set down
while the impression was still vivid.

"May 14: Olive-backed thrush—singing most softly
this morning, almost as if afraid of being heard. It is
a swooning song, and soft as it is has a vibrant penetrating quality that, as in the case of the veery's song,
cannot be held in memory. It is mystical, as if giving
expression to the unknown. It is like a crack in the
frame of this mundane world, allowing the faintest

ray of light from some outer world to come through.

"May 17: 2 olive-backed thrushes—one heard singing ever so faintly in woods south of Shoreham. Other heard and seen in ravine. Just a suggestion in the air, a whiff of song, already vanished as soon as heard.

"May 20: Olive-backed thrushes—common and singing everywhere. . . . The song is louder and fuller than a few days ago.

"May 25: 6 olive-backed thrushes in all today . . . strange, soft vibrancy of song; an atmosphere, a sort of incense in the forest. Insubstantial and evanescent, it rises like a wisp of mist through the trees in early morning.

"June 1: Olive-backed thrush? I thought I heard it in the ravine; but the song is so ghost-like and insinuating, sounding as if in the inner ear only, that it may have been just a recollection left in my imagination, based on association with the scene, as the perfume of a flower may remain after it is gone.

"June 2: Olive-backed thrush—the spirit voice of yesterday in ravine, from the same direction, only this time I made sure of it and, following up to the brink of the amphitheater, looked directly down upon my bird perched on a twig halfway down the cliff and looking up at me. Oh my darling!"

I saw my first gray-cheeked thrush of the year, and then another, on May 20 in the ravine. The second was calling *veheu* at short intervals—a call similar to the veery's but more declarative, a statement rather than a suggestion. The gray-cheek is almost identical in appearance with the olive-back. It has no eye-ring, in questionable contrast to the olive-back's often questionable eye-ring, and the feathers under the eye do not have the yellowish tinge of the olive-back's. It takes close range and a good light to be sure of these differences, but the birds haunt the shade and are generally too shy for easy approach. Consequently, it is hard to identify them surely by sight when either species may be expected. The gray-cheek, however, leaves a different impression on me in its appearance and behavior, by which I identify it instinctively, though without certainty. I generally recognize gray-cheek or olive-back as such before I have had a chance to note the distinctive markings. I should have some diffidence in setting this down here, since in certain respects my observation is opposite to that of commentators who know these birds on their nesting grounds. I speak only for a ravine in Washington, however, and on the basis of tested observation. The gray-cheek (at least the race that migrates commonly through Washington) is rangier and somewhat larger than the olive-back, which is a compact, globe-breasted bird. It seems looser of build. Moreover, it is not so flighty and elusive as the olive-back, generally allowing a closer approach without showing signs of nervousness. The olive-back, unlike its congeners, has the habit of ascending to the treetops and there engaging in fly-catching maneuvers. The gray-cheek is more strictly a groundling.

At one point along the ravine a steep slide of sand and gravel, like the path of an avalanche, makes an opening through the woods. You stand at the top, adding its height to your own (how imposing a man feels with a mountain added to him!), and survey the scene below. The sun strikes through in early morning and floodlights the foot of the slide. A man or a thrush, imagining spruce trees in place of sycamore and paulownia, might fancy himself on the slope of a lonely mountain in the far north, near timberline: an excellent place for a gray-cheek. There he was, too, the morning of May 28, singing as if he had been already on his nesting grounds up north. At first he perched in a tree at the foot of the slide, singing loudly and steadily. The song, thin of tone, consisted of an initial phrase rising in pitch, followed by a trill, then two short phrases dipping down in succession. The gray-cheek is distinguished among the spotted thrushes by its lack of distinction as a singer. How explain what utility there is in the musical loveliness of the songs sung by four out of the five species, or simply what reason there is for it, and then why the gray-cheek can dispense with it? The ancestral thrush song may have been like this, before the other thrushes, less conservative than the gray-cheek, improved on it. Not too set in its form, and lacking particular virtues, it might serve as an excellent basis for improvements.

Having greeted the day with five minutes of uninterrupted song, the gray-cheek dropped from his perch to hop about in the sunlight at the foot of the slide, and in the shadow of the adjacent trees, picking up insects. Still he sang, even as he hunted, but the volume of his voice diminished over the hours until, by late morning, it had sunk to a whisper. On other occasions, too, in the ravine, I have heard the gray-cheeks, which never sing on migration, sing. Exception to rule is the rule of life, distinguishing it from death; it is the badge of freedom.

———————————

The presence of an adult yellow-crowned night heron in the ravine on May 29, 1945, is an exception among exceptions. This species belongs to the deep South; it did not use to be found north of South Carolina, although a colony has now established itself up the Canal, near Seneca Creek.

The morning was just such a sparkler as I have described before, when the sun rises clear after a night of downpour and scatters its radiance in shafts through the mist or haze that remains in the woods. It is like the world redeemed from the Flood after the anger of God has been appeased. The sun wraps its satellite in a loving and charitable warmth. Simply to breathe the air is to be transfigured. I want for nothing this morning. I am content just to be aware of the busy life of all the common birds and insects about me, to see the movement everywhere and hear the chorus of voices. It is sad only that this moment in time cannot be retained but must evaporate like the mist itself, even from memory.

The big bird took off from shadow in the bed of the brook as I started down the ravine, hardly to be seen in its passage except confusedly through openings in the shrubbery; but I caught that straw-colored thatch on its head and knew it almost instantly for what it was. It lighted on the stub of a dead beech at the foot of the ravine and allowed me to approach until I stood within thirty feet of it, examining it through my binoculars. A shaft of sunlight fell full upon it, standing atop the stump like some emblem, alert and motionless, head high, watching me. For several minutes we gazed at each other and had each our own thoughts. Then it dropped from the stub and flapped away round the bend. In the next few days I saw the large footprints of a heron in the sandbanks along Rock Creek, but the bird itself no more.

I have always felt that the hummingbird was a special gift to the New World, since it so obviously belongs in the setting of an Oriental fairy tale. It is a fabulous creature of Ind—only it is not found in India, or anywhere outside the New World. The human imagination, which has created unicorn, dragon, and phoenix, has created nothing more wondrous. It is like a precious gem, emerald or ruby, that has life and movement, that hovers, dips, and darts in the air. Looking only at its form and color, its jeweled surface, one would say it belonged in a prince's turban. Its wings have more delicacy than the finest watchwork, humming when they are set off, whirring so fast they are blurred to sight, shooting it here and there, back and forth, or holding it stationary in the air.

May 14, in the darkest of the woods sloping down to the ravine, I watched a female hummingbird darting and hanging in air about the lower fringes of a large oak, some twenty feet aboveground. She would hang, change position, hang again . . . till suddenly she was sitting on what appeared to be a bump of lichen stuck to a horizontal branch. Thereafter I observed her about her nest almost daily until June 8, when I found it fallen to the ground. It was a small deep cup of felted material, very soft and warm. I brought it home on my thumb, and later gave it away to an English artist, a painter of birds, who took it to England with him.

———

On June 8 I saw my last spring migrant, a blackpoll warbler, behind the Japanese Embassy. This sets the terminal date for spring in Washington, 1945. I went out again June 9 and for the first time since February found no migrant; only the resident breeding birds. The accomplished fact of a Washington summer lay before me. It was already an accustomed spectacle. Frost in the air and a lone cardinal trying out his voice in a naked tree seemed far away now.

Yet this was merely one tick of the great clock that ticks out eternity. For a few ticks I am here, uncomprehending, attempting to make some record or memorial of this eternal passage, like a traveler taking notes in a strange country through which he is being hurried on a schedule not of his making and for a purpose he does not understand. He knows only that he has been bustled blindfold onto this scene and that blindfold he will be bustled off it again in short order. Meanwhile, the spectacle itself is beautiful, immense, awe-inspiring. He thinks, in default of other guidance, he had better make a few hurried notes on it in his passage. This much he must attempt, leaving his notes behind as an acknowledgment of this strange hospitality and the gift of vision, and as a record by which other travelers may recognize their similar experience.

EPILOGUE

Ten Years After

> But I have nothing more to say, replied Simmias; nor
> can I see any reason for doubt after what has been said.
> But I still feel and cannot help feeling uncertain in my
> own mind, when I think of the greatness of the subject
> and the feebleness of man.
>
> <div align="right">PLATO, <i>Phaedo</i></div>

TEN SPRINGS have passed as this Epilogue is
written. After ten springs a man should be wiser.
He should be nearer to the apprehension of that final
word by which the secret of the universe is revealed;
the word that mankind has sought through the ages;
the word that brings forth, at last, the Kingdom of God
upon Earth. It trembles on the tip of one's tongue—
and still one cannot say it. I was as close to it ten
years ago, although today I can, perhaps, tell better
what I think.

All life, I suspect, is one. There is no such thing as
the mockingbird, *Mimus polyglottos,* a species apart.
In South America the traveler sees mockingbirds that
are not quite mockingbirds, or not quite the same as
the mockingbirds he sees in Washington. There is a
spectrum of the genus *Mimus.* White in the wings
increases imperceptibly, from none at one end of the
spectrum to much at the other. Where the taxonomist
wants to draw his boundary lines, saying that everything between them constitutes one species, is a matter of his convenience. It has nothing to do with
nature. *Species* is a word, not a thing—and we should,

as Justice Holmes admonished, think things rather than words.

Genus, Family, Order, Class, and *Phylum* are equally unknown to nature. If you had before you the skins of all the birds that ever lived, laid out in a series based on kinship, you could not find any point at which that series showed a natural division. From the hummingbird to the eagle there is no break. From man to the amoeba there is no break. Only the extinction over the ages of intervening forms—gaps made by death and disappearance—has caused those apparent breaks which we see in our world of the moment.

If all the song sparrows between Maine and Arizona were to disappear, would not the first taxonomist to come along say that the Maine and Arizona birds represented, respectively, two separate species? Today we call them one species because the continuum remains between them, connecting them, making them visibly one in spite of their differences.

The ivory-billed woodpecker, today, is either already extinct or about to be. But he can be resurrected at any time by a finding of the scientists that a closely related Cuban woodpecker, instead of being a separate species, is merely a geographical variant of the same species. So our taxonomic world becomes another Wonderland for Alice.

This is the worst of our heritage from the Greek philosophers. The defect which accompanied the greatness of Socrates was in his assumption that life is made up of distinct categories. Here, he said, is The Good and there The Beautiful; here is Justice and there is Truth; here is Courage and there is Cowardice; here is the Body, there the Soul. He assumed that words like these represented actual building-blocks which God used in the Creation, and the questions he asked had to do with how these separate "ideas" combined or bore upon one another. He started the word-game that Western philosophers have played among themselves ever since, never more passionately than did the theologians of the Middle Ages who resurrected Aristotle. Socrates and Aristotle created our mockingbird.

This specialization is what will destroy our world by destroying our ability to see things whole. Either you are an Historian, today, or a Political Scientist, or a Naturalist, or some other -ist. You must make up your mind. History, in turn, is either Science or Literature, one or the other. You have to decide. And if International Relations is a category, as some now say it is, where does it belong? (How much white does it have in its wings?) Our universities are laid waste by the battles that rage over these issues.

The Philosophers have recently announced a "Revolution in Philosophy" that has occurred in the last fifty years. "Philosophers have become . . . more technical in their discourse, and more self-conscious about their own calling." They have become "conscious that philosophical problems are very different from those dealt with by their colleagues in the arts and sciences." Philosophy has been "set free" by "cutting the chains of association that traditionally had linked [it] to psychology." Philosophy has also been "set free" from metaphysics. In fact, it has been set so free from everything else that only licensed professional Philosophers, today, may read what Philosophers write. They talk to themselves in the seclusion of their own asylum.

He who writes this Epilogue is now, if you please, a Professor of Foreign Affairs. Therefore he writes it uneasily, glancing over his shoulder like a schoolboy writing a letter to his girl when he should be doing his homework. (He ought, at this moment, to be reading Chapter XXXV of Schwarzenberger's *Power Poli-*

tics, the one on "Regional and Functional Integration of the Nuclear Pattern.") Someone says he has no doctor's degree in Natural History. He is not licensed to write about Nature. But someone else points out that neither has he a degree in Foreign Affairs. Does that make it all right?—or is the case now hopeless? It will not do for him to say that he knows as much about birds as the next Professor of Foreign Affairs, or that he knows as much about Foreign Affairs as Roger Tory Peterson.

The point is that you cannot find any place to draw the line between Foreign Affairs and Nature. Let me illustrate. Everyone grants that Politics and Foreign Affairs have to do with each other. If you want to know about Politics, however, just observe a flock of crows. One of them has accidentally broken a couple of feathers in his wing. Another sees that he has and, with a raucous cry, dives upon him. The gap in the injured bird's wing puts him at a disadvantage and he can hardly defend himself. Other crows, noting his difficulty, start up a sudden self-righteous and indignant cawing. They, too, descend upon him as if they were outraged angels and he an emanation of blackness. Even his former companions can now newly perceive the defect in him, the sable stain. It becomes clear to them, too, that he must go. They, too, begin to caw and plunge bravely. The victim, especially if he has been the nonpareil of the flock, is now lucky if he can find a place of obscurity in the lower woods for the day that remains. Is this not Politics?

The man who had the greatest influence on the political thought of our age and the conduct of foreign relations was Charles Darwin, not a Political Scientist but a Naturalist.

What we need is a unified Field Theory that will embrace Einstein's equations, natural selection, the plays of Shakespeare, the Sermon on the Mount, the death of Socrates, and the behavior of crows. What we need is the one word that reveals the Kingdom of God. It trembles on the tip of the tongue—and still, after ten years, one cannot say it. But I can tell you where to look for it. Not in Schwarzenberger, and not in the President's Message on the State of the Union (unless he has broken out of his office lately). It is in the world of eternal things, the world that renews its beatitude perennially.

It occurs to me that perhaps someone has already said the word. But I did not read his book and the critic who had dismissed it as "Eschatology." There's Glory for you! Even when the word is spoken, who knows that it will not fall on deaf ears?

This, I think, is what I really want to say after ten years. Perhaps there is no secret, but we are all hard of hearing. Perhaps truth is not invisible, but we are blind.

The web of life, though seamless, has its north and south, its east and its west. There is no Good and Evil, but there is better and worse. There is a higher life and a lower—depths beneath us from which we have risen and a rarer atmosphere above the murky sea in which we live. At times we have strained upward, glimpsing filaments or sparkles of light above. This is promising. We may be farther up a million years from now, if we will keep on straining. But there is material food in the sea too, a higher standard of living lower down, and this attracts us. Today—in Politics, in Foreign Affairs, in Philosophy, even in Natural History—we look downward for the Kingdom of God. So downward we go, perhaps to remain, perhaps to perish, perhaps to rise again. Who knows?

Ten springs is not enough time. God grant us a million!

L. J. H.

The Universe
Summer, 1956.

L OUIS J. HALLE was born in New
York City. Educated at Harvard University, from 1941 to 1954 he served in the United States Department of State in various posts, and was a member of the policy planning staff. In 1954 he was appointed research professor at the University of Virginia, later joining the faculty of the Graduate Institute of International Studies in Geneva where he still teaches. He writes with authority as naturalist and political scientist, and he brings to both fields the insights of each. His books, in addition to the present volume, include *Transcaribbean, Birds Against Men* (for which he was awarded the John Burroughs Medal), *River of Ruins, On Facing the World, Civilization and Foreign Policy, Choice for Survival, Dream and Reality,* and *Of Men and Nations.*

Atheneum Paperbacks